The Catcher in the Rye

J.D. Salinger

Notes by Nigel Tookey

 Longman   York Press

YORK PRESS
322 Old Brompton Road, London SW5 9JH

ADDISON WESLEY LONGMAN LIMITED
Edinburgh Gate, Harlow,
Essex CM20 2JE, United Kingdom
Associated companies, branches and representatives throughout the world

First published 1997

ISBN 0–582–31330–9

Designed by Vicki Pacey
Illustrated by Stephen Player
Map of New York by Celia Hart
Typeset by Pantek Arts, Maidstone, Kent
Phototypeset by Gem Graphics, Trenance, Mawgan Porth, Cornwall
Produced by Longman Asia Limited, Hong Kong
Colour reproduction and film output by Spectrum Colour

CONTENTS

PREFACE

York Notes are designed to give you a broader perspective on works of literature studied at GCSE and equivalent levels. We have carried out extensive research into the needs of the modern literature student prior to publishing this new edition. Our research showed that no existing series fully met students' requirements. Rather than present a single authoritative approach, we have provided alternative viewpoints, empowering students to reach their own interpretations of the text. York Notes provide a close examination of the work and include biographical and historical background, summaries, glossaries, analyses of characters, themes, structure and language, cultural connections and literary terms.

If you look at the Contents page you will see the structure for the series. However, there's no need to read from the beginning to the end as you would with a novel, play, poem or short story. Use the Notes in a way that suits you. Our aim is to help you with your understanding of the work, not to dictate how you should learn.

York Notes are written by English teachers and examiners, with an expert knowledge of the subject. They show you how to succeed in coursework and examination assignments, guiding you through the text and offering practical advice. Questions and comments will extend, test and reinforce your knowledge. Attractive colour design and illustrations improve clarity and understanding, making these Notes easy to use and handy for quick reference.

York Notes are ideal for:

- Essay writing
- Exam preparation
- Class discussion

The author of these Notes, Nigel Tookey, is Head of English at a large Further Education college near London. He is an English graduate and a Senior Examiner for GCSE English.

The text used in these Notes is the 1994 Penguin Books edition (see Context and Setting for the history of this text).

Health Warning: **This study guide will enhance your understanding, but should not replace the reading of the original text and/or study in class.**

PART ONE

INTRODUCTION

HOW TO STUDY A NOVEL

You have bought this book because you wanted to study a novel on your own. This may supplement classwork.

- You will need to read the novel several times. Start by reading it quickly for pleasure, then read it slowly and carefully. Further readings will generate new ideas and help you to memorise the details of the story.
- Make careful notes on themes, plot and characters of the novel. The plot will change some of the characters. Who changes?
- The novel may not present events chronologically. Does the novel you are reading begin at the beginning of the story or does it contain flashbacks and a muddled time sequence? Can you think why?
- How is the story told? Is it narrated by one of the characters or by an all-seeing ('omniscient') narrator?
- Does the same person tell the story all the way through? Or do we see the events through the minds and feelings of a number of different people.
- Which characters does the narrator like? Which characters do you like or dislike? Do your sympathies change during the course of the book? Why? When?
- Any piece of writing (including your notes and essays) is the result of thousands of choices. No book had to be written in just one way: the author could have chosen other words, other phrases, other characters, other events. How could the author of your novel have written the story differently? If events were recounted by a minor character how would this change the novel?

Studying on your own requires self-discipline and a carefully thought-out work plan in order to be effective. Good luck.

Family background

J.D. Salinger was born in New York City in 1919. His full name is Jerome David Salinger. His background is not literary as his father, Sol Salinger, was in the food import business and his mother, Miriam Jillich, was a housewife. His writing is probably based on his life to some extent; some of his childhood experiences seem to link to parts of *The Catcher in the Rye* although there are no really obvious connections; he had a sister who was eight years older than him, called Doris, and no brothers.

Education

J.D. Salinger went to school in Manhattan, the same district as Phoebe's school in the novel, and his schoolwork was of average standard. At the age of thirteen he was sent to a school called the McBurney School where he lasted one year before 'flunking', just as Holden does in *The Catcher in the Rye*. At the age of fifteen his parents enrolled him in the Valley Forge Military Academy in Pennsylvania, the state where Salinger places Pencey Prep. In the novel Holden also says that his parents will probably send him to a military academy when they find out he has been expelled from Pencey Prep. J.D. Salinger successfully finished at Valley Forge in 1936.

In 1937 he joined New York University but only stayed a short while before going to Vienna with his father to learn about the family business. He came back to America after a short time and took a short story writing course. This led to his first story being published in 1940 in a magazine called *Story*.

Later life and work

During the Second World War J.D. Salinger mainly did intelligence work, but he was part of the D-day invasion force. He came back to New York at the end of the war and lived with his parents while he was writing *The Catcher in the Rye*, which was published as a serial in a magazine between 1945 and 1946; it was first published in novel form in 1951. He moved out of New

York to various places in the countryside before settling in a town called Cornish, in the state of New Hampshire. He married a woman called Claire Douglas and they now have two children. Since the popularity of *The Catcher in the Rye* and since his marriage, J.D. Salinger has been a recluse, seeking privacy and never giving interviews to the media. He refuses to talk about his fiction and will not even allow quotations to be used from his work.

The Catcher in the Rye is his only novel, but it became a classic amongst students and young people everywhere and remains so today. J.D. Salinger did write other books; all collections of his short stories were first published individually in a famous American magazine called *The New Yorker*. These include *Nine Stories*, published in 1953, and then a series of linked stories dealing with the Glass family. *Franny and Zooey* deals with the relationship between a brother and sister, strongly echoing Holden and Phoebe's relationship. The other two books are *Raise High the Roofbeam, Carpenters* and *Seymour: An Introduction* which is a series of stories about a bright but troubled young man, Seymour Glass, who eventually commits suicide.

CONTEXT & SETTING

History of the
text

The Catcher in the Rye was originally published in London in 1951 by Hamish Hamilton, and this edition and the following edition published by Penguin were different from the original American version. Minor changes were made to the original text, for instance American spellings changed to British ones, the author's use of italic removed and words taken out like 'fuck' and 'goddam', which were unacceptable to people in the 1950s.

In 1994 Hamish Hamilton and Penguin published the original American text, on which this Note is based. The use of italics in this original text gives extra emphasis to Holden's phrases, for example 'They're *nice* and all' on the first page of the novel.

Response to the novel

When first published in America by Little Brown and Co. in 1951, *The Catcher in the Rye* caused instant controversy. Many reviews said it was a sensational achievement while others objected to its use of 'bad' language and the shocking nature of some of the scenes. The novel's narrator and main character, Holden Caulfield, was also thought to be a bad example to young people. In fact the novel was banned in certain areas and some education authorities condemned it. To understand why the novel caused so much fuss, it is important to think about the time it was written and the prevailing attitudes of Americans at that time.

America's outlook

The Catcher in the Rye is set just after the Second World War; America had just played a major part in helping to win the war and had become a 'superpower'. The country was very wealthy and had a huge military force; society was affluent and very materialistic. At this time, America became the first real 'consumer society'; its people were generally well off and believed that America was the greatest country in the world.

However, America was also very conservative at this time and the people were often suspicious of anyone who was different from others, or who did not share their beliefs about American society's greatness; it was the beginning of the 'cold war' and people whose beliefs differed from the norm were often denounced as 'un-American' or 'communist sympathisers'. In *The Catcher in the Rye* Holden Caulfield rebels against some of these social attitudes and values; one small sign of this is, perhaps, Holden's red hunting hat (red being the colour associated with communism).

Rise of the
teenager

The novel can also be seen as an example of the rise of teenage rebellion. Before the 1950s there was no real notion of a 'teenager'. _The Catcher in the Rye_ dealt with teenagers' feelings towards the society in which they lived and became an instant success with students and young people. During the 1950s American teenagers started to make an identity for themselves and the decade saw the rise of Rock and Roll and teenage fashions. Young film actors like James Dean and Marlon Brando became huge stars with the films _Rebel Without a Cause_ and _The Wild Ones_. The start of the decade was in some ways the beginning of the 'generation gap' between teenagers and their parents and Holden Caulfield was one of its first spokespersons.

New York City

The Catcher in the Rye is an urban novel. It is set in a large city which acts as the background to Holden's story. When the story begins we find ourselves in the enclosed little world of a boarding school with its own rules and values. Holden 'escapes' to the world of New York City, but he often finds it a frightening place; if not frightening, then full of shallow people, or 'phonies' as he calls them. The fact that J.D. Salinger sets his novel in a real city with recognisable landmarks and buildings adds to the sense of realism (see Literary Terms) we feel when reading it. If we wished, we could go there and trace Holden's wanderings.

The city represents that which Holden sees as bad in the world; it is full of falsity and corruption. When Holden arrives in New York he immediately talks of the 'perverts' in the hotel where he stays. He has his encounter with the prostitute there and gets beaten up. All of his worst moments occur because of the city. The social world of night-clubs and bars in which he spends his time are full of uncaring people with no real moral values; no-one seems to have time for anybody else, everyone is thinking about themselves. Nearly all the

city-dwellers seem flawed in some way, as if the city has corrupted them. As Holden sees it, they all let him down when he needs them:

- Sally Hayes won't run away with him
- Carl Luce is not interested in Holden's problems
- Even Mr Antolini is perceived by Holden as making advances to him

The only exception is his sister, Phoebe, who is too young to have been influenced by the values of the city.

Central Park

The only place where Holden finds some moments of happiness is when he is in Central Park or the museums nearby. The park is a green space, a small piece of nature in a vast, man-made environment. The museums represent the past, a time when things were easier and not subject to the stresses and strains of city life. In these places Holden remembers his childhood before his brother's death and his own problems; he wishes things could stay the same as they were then. It is in the park that he finally has a moment of true happiness, when he sees his sister riding the carrousel. It is as if these places are innocent and untainted by man. In a way the park is a metaphor (see Literary Terms) for the wide open spaces to which Holden dreams of running away.

Literary traditions

Although *The Catcher in the Rye* is very much a modern, twentieth century novel, it does have links with the literary tradition of America and of Western civilisation in general. The narrative revolves around the idea of an individual battling with the values of the society in which he lives. This is quite a common theme throughout American literature, appearing in books like *The Scarlet Letter* by Nathaniel Hawthorne, *Huckleberry Finn* by Mark Twain and *Invisible Man* by Ralph Ellison.

Like some of the earliest known literature, one of the central ideas in the novel is that the main character is on a quest. However, Holden's quest does not involve

defeating strange monsters to get to his home, like the
Ancient Greek story of Ulysses, or slaying dragons
while looking for the Holy Grail, as in the stories of
King Arthur. Holden's quest is to find an answer to his
own problems; he is searching for his own lost
innocence and for a sense of moral values. He is not
like a traditional hero but rather an anti-hero (see
Literary Terms), a type of character commonly found in
twentieth-century fiction.

PART TWO

SUMMARIES

GENERAL SUMMARY

The novel concerns three days in the life of Holden Caulfield, a troubled sixteen-year-old who has been expelled from three schools. Although the main action takes place over three days, there are frequent flashbacks (see Literary Terms) to earlier events in Holden's life. It is a first-person narrative (see Literary Terms) told to us by Holden, who is recuperating from a mental breakdown in a Californian hospital. He begins by explaining that he is only going to tell us what he has told his brother, D.B., who visits him from time to time as he is working in Hollywood, near to the hospital.

Chapters 1–7:
Leaving
Pencey Prep

Holden's story begins on the day he leaves his school, a Saturday. Holden has been expelled and has to leave four days before the end of term. He begins by telling us about a farewell visit to his History teacher, Mr Spencer, and also explaining something of his own character.

We meet Ackley, the boy who has the room next to Holden's. We also meet Stradlater, Holden's roommate, who asks Holden to write a homework essay for him because he is taking a girl out that evening. Holden discovers that Stradlater's 'date' is Jane Gallagher, a girl he knows and with whom he spent a summer two years before. Holden writes the essay based on his brother Allie's baseball mitt. We find out that Allie died of leukaemia on 18 July 1946 and that Holden was very disturbed by his death. When Stradlater returns Holden gives him the essay but Stradlater is not happy with it. Holden gets upset and tears up the essay. Next, Holden asks Stradlater about his date with Jane Gallagher, becoming increasingly agitated about what Stradlater may have tried to do with her sexually. They end up fighting and this provokes Holden's early departure from school. He decides to go to New York and stay in a hotel until returning home to his parents on the Wednesday when term officially ends and when they will have received and absorbed the news of his expulsion.

Chapters 8–14: The Edmont Hotel

Holden leaves for New York by train. Whilst on the train he meets the mother of one of the students he knows at Pencey, Ernest Morrow. They talk for a while and Holden lies to her about his opinion of her son.

When he gets to New York, Holden checks in to the Edmont Hotel. He tries phoning the number of a woman given to him by an old acquaintance from school. She refuses to see him and he goes downstairs to the hotel night-club. He tells us about his younger sister, Phoebe. Holden dances with three girls before leaving and going to another night-club. In the meantime he has told us about Jane Gallagher and how fond he was of her. He still thinks about the Stradlater episode. Holden stays at the club but does not enjoy it, telling us the place was full of 'phonies'.

'Phony' is one of Holden's favourite words for describing people and places of which he has a low opinion.

After leaving the club, Holden walks back to the hotel. As he goes in he makes an arrangement with the elevator-man, Maurice, for a prostitute to be sent to his room. When she arrives Holden does not want sex. He pays her but a little later the woman and Maurice return, demanding more money. Holden refuses to pay but Maurice hits Holden and they take the money by force. At the end of this section Holden reveals to us that he feels depressed enough to kill himself.

Chapters 15–20: Faces from the past

Holden checks out of the hotel. Before doing so, he thinks about phoning Jane Gallagher but does not, instead phoning another girl he knows, Sally Hayes. They arrange to go out that afternoon. While waiting until he meets Sally, Holden meets two nuns and talks to them. He admires them and speaks of how unselfish they are. He goes to buy a record for his sister. On his way he hears a young boy singing a song that forms the basis for the novel's title. It cheers him up a little.

He takes Sally Hayes to the theatre and then on to an ice-skating rink. Holden tells Sally Hayes about his problems and asks her to run away with him, but she is unsympathetic and they part company.

Holden makes an arrangement to meet Carl Luce, a boy who used to be his student adviser at Whooton, one of the other schools Holden has attended. They talk but it is obvious that they have little in common any more. Holden has many such conversations throughout the novel, illustrating his desire to find someone to relate to and the fact that this does not really happen. His continued comments about wanting to phone Jane Gallagher also reinforce this theme.

Holden leaves the bar where he met Carl Luce and goes to Central Park; he is very drunk and drops his sister's record, which smashes. He sits in the park feeling very depressed. During this section of the novel we are frequently reminded of Holden's worsening mental state: he seems emotionally disturbed. Finally he leaves the park and decides to sneak into his parents' house and see his sister Phoebe.

Chapters 21–26: Reunited with Phoebe

Holden gets into his parents' house and finds his sister. They have a long conversation during which Phoebe realises that Holden has been expelled. She becomes very upset and Holden tries to explain himself. She accuses him of liking nothing and not wanting to do anything with his life. He tells her he wants to be a 'catcher in the rye'. Eventually Holden leaves his parents' house after making an arrangement to see Mr Antolini, one of his old teachers whom he liked, and to stay at his house until the Wednesday he is due home. Before Holden leaves he borrows his sister's Christmas savings.

When he arrives at Mr Antolini's, Holden has a long conversation with him. Mr Antolini gives Holden some serious advice about his future. Holden goes to sleep and wakes up to find Mr Antolini stroking his hair. He becomes upset and rushes out of Mr Antolini's house.

Holden decides to go away and arranges to meet his sister to give her back her money. She arrives and explains she is going with him. He realises that this cannot happen and the turning point of the novel is reached. Holden takes his sister to the park and watches her ride on a carrousel. He now feels happy and the story ends. There is one final, brief chapter where Holden tells us he will return to school next September and that he is recovering.

DETAILED SUMMARIES

CHAPTER 1   The novel opens with a young man explaining that he is going to tell us about what happened to him over one Christmas. He is in a hospital near Hollywood and is talking about his brother D.B. who is a writer and has just bought a new sports car.

The narrator says that his story began when he left his school, Pencey Prep. It was a Saturday and an American football game was being played which was important for the school. He tells us that he was not at the game but was standing on top of Thomsen Hill looking down on the action.

He was on his way to say goodbye to his History teacher. He had been expelled from school and that is the reason he had to leave. He remembers an earlier episode when he was playing football with two schoolfriends and was told to go inside by the Biology teacher, Mr. Zambesi; this sort of memory helps him to say goodbye to the school.

Note that the writer waits until the end of the chapter to reveal Holden's name.

He ran towards his History teacher's house, remembering how he stopped to catch his breath and the fierce cold. Mrs Spencer, the history teacher's wife, answers the door and it is only at this point that we discover the narrator's name is Holden. He goes into the house and asks how Mr Spencer is.

COMMENT

The first chapter sets the scene for the story and we get a sense of the character who is going to tell us the tale. We discover that the story he will tell us is only about one small part of his life, so we imagine it will be significant. In fact, the whole of the action of the novel takes place over three days, beginning on a Saturday, although Holden does spend a great deal of time recalling events from his past.

Think about how the writer develops Holden's character.

We find out about Holden's attitudes to his school and learn something about his feelings. He hates the movies and other things like advertising and publicity.

Holden comes across as an outsider. He begins the story on a hill away from everyone else. He also tells us that the fencing team would not talk to him on the way back from New York.

The most important piece of information we learn is that Holden has been kicked out of school. He has not done anything particularly bad but just seems unable to work hard enough.

Towards the end of the chapter Holden goes to say goodbye to his History teacher and this is one of the first places in the novel where we find Holden looking for companionship. He seems drawn to adults throughout the novel, as if they will help him understand his problems, but none of the encounters really works out.

GLOSSARY
David Copperfield a novel by Charles Dickens; the story of David Copperfield's life

dough money

It killed me it impressed/amused me

being a prostitute used ironically here to mean that he is prostituting his talent of writing for money

Strictly for the birds only fools would believe it

falsies a padded bra

grippe flu

CHAPTER 2

Holden tells us that Mr and Mrs Spencer are seventy years old. He goes on to describe Mr Spencer in the classroom and seems to feel sorry for him being so old. He talks about Mr Spencer getting enjoyment out of buying an old blanket from some American Indians.

At this point we find out that Holden's surname is Caulfield as this is how Mr Spencer addresses him. Holden feels sorry he has come to Mr Spencer's house and describes the medicines surrounding Mr Spencer, saying the scene makes him depressed. Mr Spencer asks Holden why he isn't at the football game and Holden explains why.

At this point Mr Spencer starts to question Holden about recent events and asks if Holden's parents know he has been expelled yet. Holden says no and then explains to Mr Spencer that Pencey Prep is the fourth school he has attended. Holden reveals to us that he is seventeen years old but sometimes acts much younger.

Give some reasons why Holden does not try at school.

Mr Spencer starts to quiz Holden about his attitude to school. Spencer tells Holden why he had to fail him in History and we learn that Holden has not really studied for any of his subjects. Spencer reads Holden's History exam answers to him which makes Holden feel uncomfortable.

y

Holden talks to Mr Spencer but at the same time is daydreaming about where the ducks in Central Park go when the lake freezes over. We discover that Holden's home is in New York. We find out the names of two of Holden's previous schools: Whooton and Elkton Hills. Holden tells us he left Elkton Hills because it was full of 'phonies'. Mr Spencer asks Holden if he is worried about his future and Holden starts to feel depressed, decides he has to go and makes an excuse to leave, lying to Mr Spencer and telling him he has to go to the gym.

COMMENT   During this chapter we find out some of Holden's own history while he is talking to his History teacher. Holden seems to have had a troubled time at school without doing anything really bad; it seems as if he just cannot be bothered. He is an unsettled and restless person and this theme of restlessness continues throughout the novel. We realise that Holden is worried *From what you* about his parents' reaction to his expulsion and get the *know of Holden so* first real inkling that Holden is unhappy; he mentions *far, note why you* being depressed three times in the chapter. Mr Spencer *think people have* seems to want to help Holden but cannot understand *trouble* him and this is how many of the people that Holden *understanding him.* meets in the novel react to him.

Keep in mind Holden's remarks about where the ducks in Central Park (see map on p. 10) go in winter; this question is repeated by Holden to various people he encounters.

GLOSSARY

Navajo an American Indian tribe

Atlantic Monthly a popular magazine of the time

shot the bull pretended to be sincere

Central Park a large park in New York

CHAPTER 3

Holden tells us he lies a lot of the time. He describes where he lived at Pencey and relates a story about Ossenburger, a man who donated a lot of money to the school. He is quite sarcastic about him and also tells us about when one of his schoolfriends farted during Ossenburger's speech.

This hat is frequently mentioned in the novel. Think about its symbolic importance.

After leaving the Spencers' house, Holden goes back to his room which he shares with Ward Stradlater. He puts on a hat and settles down to read. Holden gives us his opinion on some of the books he has read. He is interrupted by Robert Ackley, a boy who has the room next door to his. Holden describes Ackley in an unflattering way and says he is 'peculiar'. Ackley starts talking to Holden and picks up a picture of a girl called Sally Hayes who Holden used to see in New York. Holden tells Ackley about the fencing trip and Holden eventually has to give up trying to read his book as Ackley hangs around in his room. Holden starts play-acting as he knows this will annoy Ackley. Then Holden tells Ackley about where he bought his hat. He lends Ackley some scissors and complains when Ackley cuts his nails over the floor.

They go on to talk about Stradlater and which girl he is taking out that night. Ackley explains why he hates Stradlater. Holden changes the subject and complains once again about Ackley cutting his nails over the floor.

y

Stradlater comes in and asks to borrow one of Holden's jackets. At this point Ackley leaves the room. Stradlater goes to shave and Holden is left on his own.

COMMENT   In this chapter we understand more about the sort of people whom Holden thinks are phony. He dislikes Ossenburger because he tries to buy social status, and is quite scathing about his business. Again Holden reveals his schoolboyish, immature side when he tells the story about Edgar Marsalla.

When Holden tells us about his hat it does not seem to be a very important piece of information. However, this is one of the ways the writer gets us to think about Holden as someone 'different' (You might notice that Holden wears his hat much like youths today wear their baseball caps!). The hat is frequently mentioned throughout the novel.

We learn quite a lot about how Holden relates to people his own age by his descriptions of Ackley and Stradlater and their conversations. Holden likes to play the fool and we see more extreme examples of his tendency to fantasise later in the novel.

GLOSSARY   **Very big deal** important (but here said sarcastically to mean the opposite)

stiffs corpses

foils fencing-swords

The Return of the Native a novel by the author Thomas Hardy

a goner someone who is doomed

gives me a bang gives me enjoyment

hound's tooth jacket woollen, patterned jacket

CHAPTER 4   Holden goes to the bathroom to talk to Stradlater while he is shaving. Stradlater asks Holden to do him a favour and write his English homework for him which Holden thinks is ironic as he is the one being thrown out of school. Holden starts play-acting in front of Stradlater, imitating a character from a film. Stradlater asks Holden where he got his hat and then asks again if Holden will do his English homework for him. Holden says he will if he has time.

Consider the reasons why Holden gets so excited.

He quizzes Stradlater about his date for the night, asking him which girl he is taking out. When Stradlater tells him it is Jane Gallagher, Holden gets very excited as she is a girl with whom he spent some time two summers before. Holden gets more excited and tells Stradlater he feels he should go and meet her. He reveals that he used to play draughts with her all summer. Stradlater shows no interest in Holden's memories of the girl.

Holden continues to tell Stradlater he should go and say hello to Jane Gallagher but eventually decides he is not in the mood. Stradlater is still getting ready to go out while Holden keeps questioning him about where he is taking Jane. He asks Stradlater not to tell Jane that he has been expelled. Holden starts to get nervous. He seems worried about what Stradlater and Jane will get up to. We find out that Holden thinks Stradlater is rather obsessed with sex.

Ackley comes back into the room and Holden is pleased to see him as he believes it will stop him thinking about Stradlater and Jane Gallagher. Ackley stays until dinnertime.

COMMENT During Holden's meeting with Stradlater we find out that Holden is gifted at English; this idea is reinforced several times in the novel when Holden talks about the books he reads and expresses opinions on their worth. We should also remember that D.B., his brother, is a writer.

We find more evidence in this chapter of Holden's tendency to act out fantasies. Some contradictions in

Y

Holden's words become more apparent, for example that he hates the movies but likes pretending to be people in them.

Note how the author creates a link between Jane and Holden's childhood.

There is a sense of Holden yearning for a time in his past which he feels was better than now. He is nostalgic about his time with Jane Gallagher and in a way seems quite protective about her: he explains about her childhood being unhappy and worries excessively over whether Stradlater will behave when on his date with her.

GLOSSARY

Brown Betty pudding like apple crumble

can toilet/bathroom

Ziegfeld Follies a famous twenties US musical show

Vitalis an old-fashioned type of hair gel

checkers game of draughts

booze hound alcoholic

halitosis a condition which causes a bad smelling mouth

CHAPTER 5

Holden tells us about the meal at Pencey on Saturday nights and explains why the food is always steak. He goes outside after dinner with some other boys and they start playing snowballs.

Note how Holden contradicts himself by going to the movies with Ackley.

After this, Holden decides to go into town with his friend Mal Brossard for a hamburger and, possibly, to see a film. Holden asks if Mal minds Ackley joining them. They go into town but do not go to the cinema. Holden cannot be bothered to see the film and they return to Pencey early.

Ackley hangs around in Holden's room and tells a story about a girl he went out with. Holden does not believe Ackley's claims about what he and the girl got up to and wants him to go. Eventually Holden tells Ackley that he has to write Stradlater's English essay and Ackley leaves.

Holden decides to write a descriptive essay about his brother Allie's baseball glove which had poems written on it. We discover that Holden's brother died of leukaemia on 18 July 1946. Holden talks fondly of him and says how intelligent and well-liked he was by everyone. We find out how badly affected Holden was by his brother's death; his parents were going to send him to a psychiatrist after he broke all the windows in the family's garage. Holden tells us that his hand was damaged and has never fully healed.

Holden writes the essay and then stares out of the window telling us he could hear Ackley snoring. He describes all of Ackley's ailments and says he feels sorry for him.

COMMENT

Note other examples of Holden saying one thing and then the opposite.

Once again we find Holden contradicting himself, continuing to say he hates the movies but being prepared to go there. Most of the time he complains about Ackley and deliberately tries to annoy him, yet he asks if Ackley wants to go to the movies. This is one way the writer conveys the sense that Holden is a rather mixed-up young man, unsure of what he really thinks.

The introduction into the story of the subject of Holden's dead brother is crucial. Holden's description of his brother makes Allie sound almost perfect and Holden's actions after his death seem out of his own control; he is enraged that his brother has died when he seemed such a good person. We can imagine that Allie's death was perhaps the point when Holden started to do badly at school. In several instances later in the novel when Holden is frightened or depressed he holds imaginary conversations with his dead brother. This device is used by J.D. Salinger to keep reminding us of the importance of Allie's death to Holden and it creates a strong sense of this event's continuing effect on Holden's state of mind.

In this chapter we realise that Holden is not as cynical as he has appeared so far. He does have a caring side, revealed when he tells us about his brother and when he feels sorry for Ackley.

GLOSSARY **hydrant** water-point for firefighters
Cary Grant popular American film star of the 1940s and 1950s
Buick American make of large car
baseball mitt special glove used by fielders in baseball

CHAPTER 6

Holden, as narrator, is trying to remember what happened when Stradlater returned from his date with Jane Gallagher. There are some details that Holden cannot remember, like where he was sitting when Stradlater came in.

Stradlater returns and asks Holden if he has written his English essay for him. When he has read it he complains to Holden that it is not the type of essay he asked for and gets very angry with Holden. Holden takes the essay from Stradlater, tears it up and throws the pieces into a rubbish bin.

Holden lights a cigarette to annoy Stradlater who then complains. Holden ignores him. They start talking about Stradlater's date with Jane. Holden tells us how much he hated Stradlater at this point. Holden becomes very worried about what has happened between Stradlater and Jane and accuses Stradlater of having sex with her in the car which he borrowed from Ed Banky, the school basketball coach.

Consider why Holden does not remember this incident very well.

Holden remembers vaguely that he tried to hit Stradlater but missed. Stradlater pins Holden down and tries to calm him, but Holden starts insulting Stradlater. When Holden refuses to keep quiet, Stradlater hits him and gives him a nose bleed.

Stradlater leaves the room because Holden keeps calling him names. Holden puts on his red hat and looks at his face in the mirror. He explains he has only been in two fights before and 'lost' them both. He goes into Ackley's room.

COMMENT

There are two things in this chapter which make Holden lose his temper with Stradlater. One is the complaint about the English essay and the second is his concern about Jane Gallagher.

Holden tears up the essay in anger because Stradlater has shown no gratitude for his efforts but also, perhaps, because it has brought back painful memories about his brother Allie.

Do you think Holden's attack on Stradlater was caused by jealousy?

His concern about Jane could be thought of as a jealous reaction. He hates the idea of someone he likes being with someone else. Holden also seems concerned about Jane losing the innocence she had when he knew her and thinks that Stradlater will corrupt her in some way. He comes across like the concerned father of a teenage daughter. We are reminded here of when, in Chapter 2, Holden tells us at times he acts younger than his age and sometimes older. Eventually he loses control of his emotions and swings at Stradlater, even though he has already mentioned that Stradlater is older and stronger than he is.

GLOSSARY

socks punches
faculty guys teachers' assistants
Give her the time have sex with her

CHAPTER 7

When Ackley sees all the blood on Holden's face, he asks him what has happened. Holden explains briefly and asks Ackley if he wants to play cards. Ackley persists in asking Holden for more details about the fight but Holden refuses to tell him. Instead he lies and tells Ackley that he was fighting Stradlater on his behalf, but quickly admits he is kidding.

y

Holden talks about sex in very vague terms. Give reasons for this.

Holden lies down on Ackley's roommate's bed and tells us he feels lonely. He starts to imagine Jane and Stradlater in the car and becomes very depressed. Ackley falls asleep but Holden lies awake. He tells us a story about when he went out with Stradlater and two girls and how Stradlater tried to seduce one of them.

Feeling lonely again, Holden wakes Ackley up to talk about how to join a monastery. When Ackley gets annoyed Holden says goodbye to him sarcastically. He decides to leave Pencey right then and rent an hotel room in New York, instead of waiting until the end of term three days later. He thinks about what his mother will say when she gets the headmaster's letter saying he has been expelled.

What do you think is the effect on the reader of Holden's admission of guilt?

Holden packs his bags and feels guilty when he packs the new ice-skates his mother sent him. He counts his money and decides to wake up a schoolfriend to get more money by selling his typewriter. He leaves the school, shouting an insult to the sleeping students.

COMMENT

During this chapter Holden reveals a lot about the way he feels. He does not seem to have any real friends. Even though he goes to Ackley's room after the fight, he is sarcastic towards him and tells us he is stupid. Perhaps Holden wants some sympathy and kindness but Ackley is not sensitive to this.

Holden's memory of happy times with Jane has been spoilt by Stradlater and he cannot get the image of Stradlater with Jane out of his mind. This affects him a great deal and is the main reason for his early departure from Pencey.

The idea of Holden as a 'loner' is given added weight by the writer. The last person Holden sees at Pencey is Ackley, someone who has no friends at school and who is different from the others. While Holden professes a

dislike of Ackley he also feels sorry for him. It is as if
Holden realises that no-one cares about Ackley, just as
he feels no-one cares about himself.

GLOSSARY   **Canasta** a card game

    killed me here means annoyed me; in the following chapter it is
       used to mean amused again

    Abraham Lincoln American president famous for his speeches

    Gladstones travelling bags

Identify the following characters.

1 The teacher Holden visits.
2 The people Holden goes out with in Chapter 5.

Locate the following information.

3 How many schools Holden refers to.
4 What amuses Holden during Ossenburger's speech.
5 What Holden's composition is about.
6 Why Holden feels sorry for Ackley.
7 Why Holden loses his temper with Stradlater.

Check your answers on page 89.

Consider these issues.

a How the author builds up Holden's character.

b The way Holden talks about his school.

c Which of the people whom Holden talks about he likes, if any.

d What Holden has revealed about his feelings.

e How the author builds up Holden and Stradlater's confrontation.

THE EDMONT HOTEL

CHAPTER 8 On leaving Pencey, Holden walks to the station and catches a train to New York. He tells us that he usually enjoys train journeys. After Holden has been on the train for a short time a woman gets on. She is the mother of Ernest Morrow, one of the students Holden knew at Pencey.

The woman notices a Pencey Prep sticker on Holden's luggage and strikes up a conversation with him about the school. Holden tells us that her son was one of the students he most disliked but he pretends to the woman that he liked him. Holden lies about his name to Mrs Morrow and tells her it is Rudolph Schmidt, the name of the school caretaker.

Holden notices the woman's jewellery and goes on to say she is attractive. He tells us he likes her and begins to feel guilty about lying to her.

Think of Holden's reasons for asking Mrs Morrow for a drink.

The conversation with Mrs Morrow carries on and Holden tells her that he and some of the other boys wanted to elect Ernest class president. Holden invites Mrs Morrow for a drink. He tells her he can get served because he has some grey hair, making him look older than he is. She tells him the bar will be closed.

Mrs Morrow asks Holden why he is going home before the end of term and Holden lies again, telling her he has to have an operation on a small brain tumour. Mrs Morrow is horrified but Holden says it isn't serious. They say goodbye and she invites him to spend some of the summer with her and Ernest; Holden tells us this is the last thing he would want to do.

COMMENT

Consider Holden's motives for lying.

We find more evidence in this chapter of Holden's tendency to lie. This seems closely linked with the way he play-acts. His lies to Mrs Morrow are to protect himself but also to make her feel good about her son.

This is the first meeting with an adult after Holden has left Pencey. Notice how Holden tries to act like an adult, or at least how he thinks an adult would act. He offers her cigarettes and invites her for a drink.

Holden is complimentary to Mrs Morrow, even though he is informing us how much he dislikes her son. We could think Holden insincere, something he accuses other people of being when he calls them 'phonies'.

GLOSSARY   **lousy with rocks**   wearing a lot of jewellery

                 president of the class   American equivalent of head prefect

CHAPTER 9   When Holden arrives in New York the first thing he wants to do is phone someone but he cannot decide who to phone. He takes a taxi but absent-mindedly gives his home address; he tells the taxi driver he has made a mistake. Holden asks the driver about the ducks on the lake in Central Park but the driver just thinks he is strange. Holden tells the driver to take him to the Edmont Hotel, taking off his red hat before checking in.

Holden is given a room overlooking the other side of the hotel, but he says he is too depressed to care. He describes a man dressing up in women's clothes, who he can see in one of the rooms opposite. He also sees a man and a woman squirting water at each other from their mouths. Holden calls them 'perverts' and says he is the only normal person there. He thinks of Stradlater, saying he would love the hotel.

Note how the writer uses the topic of sex to show us Holden's immaturity.   Holden thinks about his feelings regarding sex and admits he doesn't understand it. He considers ringing Jane Gallagher but says he isn't in the mood. Holden feels like meeting a woman and remembers a phone number of a woman he thinks used to be a stripper, given to him by an acquaintance.

Although it is very late Holden phones the woman, who is angry at being woken. When she finds out that Holden's acquaintance went to an expensive private college she becomes more friendly but still will not come out that night. She asks Holden if she can meet him the next night but he refuses. Immediately he regrets it but they hang up. He thinks he has handled the situation badly.

COMMENT   The topic of the ducks on the lake is mentioned again. The writer creates an image (see Literary Terms) of escape by this detail, which could represent Holden's own 'flight' from school.

Holden's views on women and sex form quite a large part of this chapter. He seems confused and, in one way, repelled by sexual activity. The people he sees from his room disgust him and his own attempts to persuade the girl on the phone out for cocktails fail. This is all evidence of Holden's struggle to deal with the period between childhood and adulthood.

The idea that Holden seems desperate for company is reinforced by his:

Consider the reasons for Holden seeking company.

- Wanting to phone someone from the station
- Asking the taxi driver if he would like a cocktail with him, even though he has never seen him before
- Phoning the girl so late at night

GLOSSARY   **screwball** weirdo
highballs cocktails, for example whisky and soda
Princeton a very prestigious American college

CHAPTER 10

Holden decides to go down to the hotel night-club, the Lavender Room. While changing he thinks about phoning Phoebe, his little sister, but is too frightened of his parents answering.

Y

Notice that Phoebe also tells stories, just like Allie, D.B. and Holden.

Holden, speaking affectionately about his sister, tells us that she is pretty and understanding. He mentions her favourite film, *The 39 Steps*, and tells us she knows the dialogue by heart. He says she likes to write stories. Holden remembers when he and his brother Allie used to take her to the park and how much Allie liked her.

Holden enters the Lavender Room and tries to buy an alcoholic drink but is refused. He starts talking to three girls, offering to dance with them one at a time. One of them dances with him and he tells us what a good dancer she was. While Holden is dancing with her he tries to talk to her but she is not interested. They sit down and Holden gives his name as Jim Steele. Holden tells us he danced with all three of the girls and that one of them was a bad dancer. To amuse himself, he pretends to have seen a movie star in the club. The girl returns to her friends and repeats what Holden has just told her, which amuses him.

Think about whether Holden realises he is being teased.

Holden buys the girls two drinks each before the bar closes. One of the girls teases Holden about his age and shortly after this they leave. He pays the bill and is aggrieved that the girls did not offer anything towards the drinks but then says he wouldn't have accepted their money anyway. He leaves the Lavender Room.

Comment

The memories of Phoebe, which occupy Holden's thoughts at the beginning of the chapter, make us think of her as a symbol (see Literary Terms) for him of what was good about family life. However, he is still too afraid of his parents' reactions to risk phoning home. Holden's urge to see Phoebe becomes stronger as the story progresses.

When Holden orders a drink and is refused service, we realise how easy it is for people to see he is just a young man and not the 'adult' he tries to be.

*Do you think
Holden's attitudes
towards girls are
typical for a boy of
his age?* We find more evidence of the contradictions between
what Holden reveals to us and what he says to the
people he meets. He is polite to the girls he meets and
seems to want to spend time with them, but he
constantly tells us what 'morons' they were. The
encounter could also be seen as more evidence of
Holden's loneliness.

GLOSSARY   **killed** used here to mean liked/amused

grools stupid, ugly people

no can no bottom

jitterbug popular dance in the 1940s and 1950s

toleja told you

ice-cold hot licks poor trumpet solos

the check the bill

Radio City Music Hall a famous venue for live performances

CHAPTER 11

As Holden goes into the hotel lobby he starts to think
of Jane Gallagher again. The thought of her and
Stradlater in the car still upsets him.

*Why do you think
it is significant
that Holden has
shown Jane his
brother's baseball
mitt?* He talks about when he got to know Jane and how they
spent a summer together. Holden describes Jane's
appearance and reveals that she is the only other person
to whom he has shown Allie's baseball mitt.

Holden tells us about a specific incident when he and
Jane came close to kissing. The story involves Jane
getting upset about her stepfather, Mr Cudahy. Holden
describes him as a 'booze-hound' and says how Jane
refused to speak to him and how when he left she
started crying. Holden tried to comfort her and in the
process started kissing her face but, he stresses, not on
her mouth.

Holden explains that Jane was a warm and affectionate
person and different from other girls. He talks about
going to the movies with her. As he is thinking about

this, the memory of her and Stradlater returns again. Even though Holden is sure Jane would not have done anything physical with Stradlater, the thought still upsets him.

Holden is not tired and decides to get a taxi to a night-club called Ernie's where his brother D.B. used to go before moving to Hollywood. He tells us about the piano player at the club.

COMMENT   Nearly the whole of the chapter is taken up with Holden's memories of Jane. Once again, we see Holden being nostalgic about the past when life seemed better for him.

Holden seems to be in love with Jane. Do you agree?

The writer reveals to us Holden's caring side, showing him to be a complex character. Holden is still genuinely concerned about Jane and remembers fondly their time together. He seems to have a lot in common with her; for example, they both have unhappiness in their childhood, she is 'different' just like Holden and they enjoy doing the same things together.

GLOSSARY   **gave me the big freeze** ignored me
Maine/Cape Cod seaside resorts near New York
glider swinging sun-chair covered with an awning
Greenwich Village a 'trendy' district of New York

CHAPTER 12

Holden gets in the taxi and says how depressing the city looks from the streets. He wishes he could go home and see his sister Phoebe. He starts talking to the driver about the ducks on the lake. The driver says he does not know the answer but begins a strange conversation about what happens to the fish in the lake during winter. Holden invites the driver for a drink even though he has told us he is the 'touchiest guy' he has ever come across. The driver refuses.

Think about reasons why Holden stays in the club despite not liking it.

On entering the club, Holden tells us it is packed with college students. He talks about Ernie, the piano player, whom he has already described in Chapter 11, saying he was messing up the song being played but that the audience still loved it. He thinks the situation is 'phony' and it depresses him; however, he does not leave because he does not want to be alone.

Holden is shown to a bad table but is served with alcohol. He explains that no-one there cares about underage drinking.

Holden sits and listens to people's conversations, telling us they are all 'jerks'. He dislikes everything he hears. Suddenly, one of his brother's old girlfriends, Lillian Simmons, appears and starts talking to Holden about his brother. She introduces her boyfriend and invites Holden to join them for a drink. Holden refuses and lies to her, saying he has to meet someone. He leaves the club.

COMMENT

Note that Chapter 11 ends by Holden deciding to take a taxi and describing Ernie at the club, and then Chapter 12 begins by jumping back to the taxi-ride on the way to the club. This use of flashback (see Literary Terms) is typical of a conversational, episodic story (see Literary Terms and Structure).

The events in the taxi are almost identical to the previous ride Holden took. What is different is that this driver engages him in conversation. Holden argues about the fish in the lake but gives up because the driver seems to be angry. In a way, the conversation indicates how Holden tries to communicate with people but often fails. He is misunderstood in more ways than one.

Identify what Holden thinks is phony about the club.

After seeing the caring side of Holden in the last chapter we witness more of his sarcastic side in the night-club. He is scathing about all aspects of the club, complaining that everything about the place is phony. He claims it depresses him, just as the streets of New York have done earlier.

Holden complains about being on his own in the club but when someone invites him to join them he refuses; he seems awkward and does not want to talk about his brother. In this chapter our impression of Holden as an outsider is made stronger by the writer contrasting his dislike of the club with the fact that everyone else there is enjoying themselves.

GLOSSARY

tossed his cookies was sick

Tattersall vests smart-looking waistcoats

Ivy League collective name for students of the five most expensive American colleges based near New York

crocked drunk

CHAPTER 13

Holden walks back quite a distance to the hotel. He tells us again how cold it was and starts daydreaming about what he would have said to whoever stole his gloves at Pencey. He pretends briefly that he would have acted tough but admits he is a bit of a coward and would probably have done nothing.

Link Holden's depression here to other parts of the novel.

These thoughts make him depressed and he decides to stop off for another drink. He brags about how much he can drink saying it doesn't affect him, but decides against going into the bar.

When he gets back to the hotel, he feels very depressed. He gets in the elevator where the person operating it asks him if he wants a woman for the night. Holden lies about his age, saying he's twenty-two, and accepts the offer. He tells us it is against his principles but that he was too depressed to think straight. The man says he will send the girl up to Holden's room in fifteen minutes, after having told him it will cost five dollars.

Holden waits in his room and changes his clothes. He admits that he is a virgin and tells us he is nervous. He thinks about a book he once read about someone who was a womaniser but says he wouldn't be like that.

The prostitute arrives and Holden quickly realises she is about the same age as him. Holden tells her he is twenty-two but she does not believe him. As they talk the girl pulls her dress off, which shocks Holden. He feels embarrassed and 'peculiar' and tries to make conversation with the girl. She is not interested in talking and Holden finally admits he doesn't feel like sex. He makes up a story that he has recently had an operation and then pays the prostitute. She says to him he should give her ten dollars but Holden says the elevator-man said five. She leaves the room.

COMMENT   Holden talks about his depression more and more as this section of the novel progresses. It is these feelings of sadness and loneliness which lead to him agreeing to see the prostitute. Holden seems to think that if he does things which are supposed to be enjoyable and which he associates with being an adult male then his depression will go away: this also explains his outings to night-clubs and his drinking.

Look at how the author portrays Holden's feelings when he is waiting for the prostitute.

The scene with the prostitute gives us an important insight into Holden's moral attitudes. He accepts the elevator-man's offer of a prostitute because he wants to appear as a carefree 'man about town', enjoying life and with money to spend. Almost as soon as he has done this he regrets it and we find out about his innocence with regard to sex.

When the prostitute arrives and Holden sees how young she is, he feels sorry for her. Holden sees her world as sad and corrupt. He realises he cannot have sex with her and vaguely describes his feelings. It is as if he does not know the words to describe his emotions at that moment and this shows his innocence again.

His attempts to have a conversation with the girl fail, reinforcing the idea that Holden wants to communicate meaningfully with someone but cannot. This theme of his inability to connect with anyone (see Theme on Relationships) runs through most of the novel. With one or two exceptions, nobody he meets seems interested in him as a person.

Holden's tendencies to act out fantasies are shown again in this chapter. He pretends to be a 'tough guy' at the beginning of the chapter and tries, but fails, to act like a 'macho' man in the scene with the prostitute.

GLOSSARY   **yellow** a coward

a little tail sex with a woman

a throw one act of sexual intercourse

CHAPTER **14**

Holden sits in his room; it is dawn on Sunday morning. He feels very depressed and starts an imaginary conversation with his brother Allie.

Consider why Holden thinks about religion here.

After Holden has got into bed he starts telling us his views on the Bible; he reveals that he likes Jesus but not the disciples and tells us he is an atheist.

There is a knock on Holden's door. It is Maurice, the elevator-man, and the prostitute, Sunny, who demand more money from Holden. He refuses to pay and Maurice threatens him. Holden says he will call the police but Maurice dissuades him, asking him if he would want his parents to know he had been with a prostitute. While Holden struggles with Maurice, Sunny finds Holden's wallet and takes out the extra five dollars they are demanding. Holden starts crying and

calls Maurice a 'moron'. Maurice and the girl leave after he has punched Holden in the stomach.

Holden lies on the floor as he did when Stradlater hit him. He then walks to the bathroom, telling us he was in a lot of pain. He goes into another of his fantasies, pretending to have been shot in the stomach and then getting his revenge by shooting Maurice. He blames his fantasising on the movies.

At the end of the chapter Holden tells us he is so depressed he feels like killing himself.

COMMENT Holden's imaginary conversation with Allie represents an attempt to counter his depression. He imagines putting right a time when he let his brother down.

The subject of Jesus, which occurs so soon after Holden's encounter with the prostitute, could be seen as a way of introducing Holden's guilt at what he has done. He knows his actions are 'sinful' according to the Bible and, even though he claims to be an atheist, the introduction of religion into his thoughts is significant.

The idea that Holden is a boy in a man's world is reinforced by the fight scene with Maurice. Holden cannot stop Maurice and Sunny taking the money and his reactions are those of a child: he cries and hurls insults, just as he did with Stradlater.

Holden's comments at the end of the chapter reveal how desperate he has become. The events that have taken place over the Saturday night reveal Holden to be a very young man who cannot cope with the adult world he is trying to inhabit and who is saddened by the people he meets.

GLOSSARY   **BB guns** ball-bearing guns

                     chisel me con me

                     plugged shot

                     rubbernecks people with an unhealthy interest in others' affairs

Identify the following characters.

1 The woman Holden meets on the train to New York.
2 The girls with whom Holden dances.
3 The piano player at the club.
4 The prostitute Holden sees.

Locate the following information.

5 The names of the night-clubs Holden visits.
6 Where Holden and Jane spent time together.
7 The reason for Holden's fight with the elevator-man.

Check your answers on page 89.

Consider these issues.

a The reasons behind Holden's lying.

b The way the author reveals aspects of Holden's past to us.

c How other characters react to Holden when he attempts to converse with them.

d The way Holden describes the Edmont Hotel.

e Holden's behaviour in the clubs which he visits.

f Our reaction to Holden's depression and loneliness.

g The way the author presents the scene with the prostitute.

h Whether we have sympathy for Holden after he is hit by Maurice.

CHAPTER **15**

At ten o'clock Holden wakes up and feels hungry but does not send out for any food as he is frightened that Maurice may bring it. He thinks about phoning Jane but again decides that he is not in the mood.

Holden phones Sally Hayes and arranges to meet her at two o'clock. He checks out of the hotel and takes a taxi to Grand Central Station to leave his bags in the left luggage facility. On the way there he gives us a little information about his father and mother, telling us that his father is a wealthy lawyer and that his mother has not been well since Allie's death.

Notice that this is the first mention of any detail about Holden's parents.

While having breakfast at the railway station, Holden meets two nuns and gives them ten dollars towards charity. He starts a conversation with them. He discovers that one is an English teacher and they talk for quite a while about books Holden has read. They discuss *Romeo and Juliet*.

When the nuns have gone, Holden tells us he enjoyed talking to them. Holden wishes he had given the nuns a bigger donation and tells us that money makes you miserable.

COMMENT

Once again, Holden thinks about phoning Jane but does not. We sense that he is frightened that by talking to her now it will spoil his memories of her. He could also be worried about what she may say about her and Stradlater. When Holden makes a date with Sally Hayes it seems as though she is a substitute for the person Holden really wants to see.

Think about why Holden keeps putting off phoning Jane.

We see Holden's generosity in his donation to the nuns. Money seems unimportant to him – perhaps because of his wealthy father?

The conversation with the nuns is one of the few in the novel where Holden is himself and not putting on an act or lying. This could be the reason why he enjoys talking to them.

Holden reveals more to us about his knowledge of English literature when he talks about *Romeo and Juliet*. It makes us wonder again why an intelligent young person should keep getting thrown out of school, the reason for his current plight.

GLOSSARY   **freshman** first-year university student
West Point cadet student at famous American military academy
Grand Central Station main railway station in New York
blue as hell really miserable

CHAPTER 16

Holden thinks about the nuns and tries to imagine his mother or his friends' mothers working for charity. He says they would only do it if it brought them attention and tells us he admires the nuns.

Consider why the boy singing makes Holden less depressed.

Holden goes to buy a record called *Little Shirley Beans* for his sister. On his way to the shop a family is walking in front of him. Their son, a boy of six, is singing a song with the lyrics, 'If a body catch a body, coming through the rye'. When Holden hears this he feels less depressed.

After he has bought *Little Shirley Beans* for his sister, Holden decides to phone Jane. He gets through but her mother answers and he puts the phone down, saying he wasn't in the mood to talk to her.

Holden buys tickets to a musical for himself and Sally Hayes. He gives us his views on the theatre and tells us about when his brother D.B. took him and his sister to see *Hamlet*. He goes on to the park to look for Phoebe but she is not there.

He decides to walk across the park to the Museum of Natural History (see map on p. 10) and on his way remembers one of his teachers, Miss Aigletinger, taking his junior class there. He talks about seeing a Columbus exhibition and passing through the room containing American Indian exhibits and models of their activities. On reaching the museum, Holden decides he cannot face going in and leaves in a taxi to meet Sally.

COMMENT

Holden's thoughts about the nuns give us more information about his values. The nuns are poor but are doing something which Holden sees as worthwhile and good. He sees rich people's attitudes to charity as a way of drawing attention to themselves. They are doing something good but for the wrong reasons.

Think of the reasons why the title is based on such a minor incident.

The short scene when Holden hears the little boy singing is one of only two places in the novel where the author alludes to the title. The other reference is in Chapter 22.

Holden is beginning to think about his family more and more. He knows the likelihood of finding his sister in the park is slim, but something drives him to go there.

Holden's mood swings between happiness and depression. This is a sign that he is becoming rather unstable.

The comments about the museum exhibits indicate that Holden likes things to stay as they are. He feels secure knowing that the museum will not change, even though individuals will. We can compare his thoughts on the museum to the way Holden wants his memories of Jane Gallagher to remain unspoilt, and also with his memories of childhood when Allie was alive.

GLOSSARY

Broadway main street in New York, famous as centre of music business (see map on p. 10)

Dixieland traditional jazz style

Flys Up a ball game

CHAPTER 17

Holden arrives at the Biltmore, where he meets Sally Hayes. He tells us he feels like marrying her as soon as he sees her, because she looks so pretty. She is pleased when he tells her and they start kissing in the taxi and he tells her that he loves her.

They go to the show and Holden tells us that it wasn't too bad. He relates the plot, giving his opinions on the quality of the acting. During the interval they go out for a cigarette and Holden comments on the number of phonies there. Sally sees a boy she knows and spends the interval period talking to him instead of Holden. This upsets Holden.

Consider why Holden decides to spill out his problems to Sally.

After the show Holden and Sally go ice-skating at Radio City. He tells us they were the worst skaters on the rink and they go and sit down. Sally asks Holden if he will come to her house on Christmas Eve to decorate the Christmas tree. Holden changes the subject and asks Sally if she ever gets fed up. He tells her what he hates about his life but she is not sympathetic. He asks her to run away with him but this frightens her and she tells him he is shouting at her. Holden tells Sally she is a 'pain in the ass' and she starts crying. He apologises but she is still upset. Eventually he leaves without her.

Holden tells us he doesn't know why he asked Sally to run away with him, saying he wouldn't have taken her even if she had agreed to go. He tells us that paradoxically he meant what he said to her at the time.

COMMENT

We find out how impulsive Holden can be, which is another sign of his immaturity. His desire to marry Sally, just because she looked attractive, demonstrates this side of his character. As he tells her he loves her, he is telling us that his actions are crazy.

y

There is more information given about the things Holden thinks are phony. Many of the things he 'hates' are based on what he sees as insincerity. He thinks that many people he knows are shallow and false, unlike the nuns.

Think about other parts of the novel where 'escape' from difficult situations is suggested.

For the first time in the novel Holden tries to convey how he really feels to someone of his own age. He tells Sally about a lot of his fears and 'hates', but she cannot understand his problems. Once again, Holden has tried to explain his state of mind and failed. At this point in the novel he does not seem to be able to relate to anyone. Even though Sally is not sympathetic to Holden's feelings, he still asks her to run away with him. She thinks his suggestions are ridiculous and says so. We can see from this dialogue how Sally is a settled member of society, quite happy with the world she lives in. However, Holden seems more and more of an outsider and also increasingly desperate to find a solution or a way out of his problems.

We discover from Sally's remarks that Holden is shouting and getting excitable, even though he seems unaware of it. This tendency is also mentioned in Chapter 19. It is a sign that Holden finds it hard to control his behaviour.

GLOSSARY **corny** unfashionable
rubbering looking around at people
vests jackets

CHAPTER 18

After Holden leaves the skating-rink he thinks about phoning Jane again. He remembers seeing her at a dance with a boy called Al Pike, whom he did not like. He is puzzled by what girls see in boys like Al.

He phones Jane but there is no reply. He phones an old acquaintance from school, Carl Luce, and arranges to meet him after telling us there are only three people in his address book: Jane, an old teacher called Mr Antolini, and his father at the office.

Think of reasons for Holden's lengthy discussion of the film.

While Holden is waiting to meet Carl Luce, he goes to the movies. Before the film comes on there is a live Christmas show which he dislikes. He explains the plot of the film to us in detail, telling us it was set in wartime, and says it was phony.

After the film, Holden goes to meet Carl Luce. On the way, he thinks about war films and tells us that D.B. was in the Second World War. Holden explains that he would hate being in the army and would rather die than go to war.

COMMENT

Yet again we see Holden exhibiting jealousy over an episode from his past which involved Jane. Once more, he fails to contact her. We get the feeling that he is not destined to speak to her and that the one person who could help him will not be available.

There is more evidence of Holden saying one thing and doing another when he goes to the movies to kill time before meeting Carl. He has told us several times how much he dislikes the movies. Perhaps this could be linked to the fact that his brother went away to work in Hollywood.

Holden's thoughts about the war would have been quite shocking at the time the novel was published, because America was very proud of its army and its role in the war. This is another way in which Holden is rebelling against the values of the society in which he lives.

GLOSSARY

homey ordinary

on furlough for a short break

A Farewell to Arms famous book by Ernest Hemingway set in the First World War

The Great Gatsby well-known American novel by F. Scott Fitzgerald

Y

CHAPTER 19

Holden is in the Wicker Bar where he has arranged to meet Carl Luce. He tells us that it is full of phonies. As Carl Luce arrives, Holden informs us that he used to be his student adviser and that he and some other boys used to meet in Luce's room to discuss sex.

Do you think Luce's meeting with Holden is like others in the novel? Luce and Holden have a conversation which mainly revolves around Holden asking questions about Luce's girlfriends. Luce tells Holden he is going out with a Chinese sculptress, which fascinates Holden. Eventually, Luce tells Holden to stop asking questions about her. The conversation moves on to Holden telling Luce about his sex life, which he explains is terrible. We find out that in the past Luce has suggested to Holden that he sees a psychoanalyst. Luce gets up to leave and Holden pleads with him to stay for one more drink. Luce refuses and departs.

COMMENT

Almost the whole chapter is taken up by Holden's conversation with Luce. It is like many others in the novel; Holden irritates Luce who obviously finds him immature. We also find Luce telling Holden he is shouting. This time, unlike with Sally, Holden admits he talks loudly when he is excited.

It is significant that Holden chooses to meet his old student adviser. He is looking for help and companionship, but Luce has grown up and changed.

A lot of the conversation is about Holden's preoccupation with sexual relationships; sexuality is becoming increasingly important to him. He reveals his immaturity by his childish questions.

Holden is still frightened of being on his own, as we see from the way he asks Luce to stay. Holden does not really know what to do; it is late on Sunday night and he has nowhere to stay.

FACES FROM THE PAST

GLOSSARY   **snowing hell** flattering excessively
                flits homosexuals
                Columbia large New York university
                the Village Greenwich Village (see map on p. 10)

CHAPTER 20

Holden stays in the Wicker Bar, getting more and more drunk. As he sits there he starts pretending he has been shot again. He decides to phone Jane but, again, he says he isn't in the mood and phones Sally Hayes instead.

After speaking to Sally's grandmother, Holden has a drunken conversation with Sally and promises to go to her house on Christmas Eve; Sally tells him he is drunk and that he should go home to bed. Holden regrets phoning her.

Holden tries to sober himself up in the washroom by dunking his head in a sink full of water. He has a brief conversation with the piano player, who also tells him to go home.

Think about why the image of the ducks has been used again here. When he has left the bar, Holden starts crying and tells us he is very depressed and lonely. He decides to go to the park and look for the ducks on the lake. He is worried about where he will sleep.

When he gets to the park, Holden drops Phoebe's record and it breaks. This makes him more depressed. He has trouble finding the lake and sits down on a park bench. He imagines what his funeral would be like if he died and feels sorry for his mother and father. He tells us the only good thing would be that his little sister would not be allowed to go to his funeral because she is too young. Holden goes on to talk about visiting his brother Allie's grave with his parents and says how much it upset him. Eventually Holden decides to sneak home and see his sister Phoebe.

COMMENT   When Holden phones Sally it seems again that she is a substitute for the person he really wants to talk to. Once more he has tried to communicate with someone at an inappropriate moment. His conversation with the piano player is also 'unfriendly'.

The events in this chapter mark the low point of Holden's experiences so far in the novel. He has reached the end of his tether! He has no money left, he is cold, drunk and rather frightened.

Try to locate other places in the novel which are about death.   Holden's feelings at this point are powerfully brought across by the writer. His thoughts of dying, of visiting his brother's grave, and even his drunken play-acting about being shot, are all reinforcing the sense we get of Holden's fears and depression.

Holden's decision to go home and see his sister is very risky, in terms of getting caught by his parents. Perhaps Holden wants to 'get caught' but cannot admit it?

GLOSSARY   **jerk** fool
singles one dollar bills
quarters twenty-five cent coins
nickel five cent coin

TEST YOURSELF (Chapters 15–20)

Identify the following characters.

1 The girl whom Holden takes to the theatre.

2 Holden's junior school teacher.

3 The main actors in the show which Holden goes to with Sally.

4 The old schoolfriend with whom Holden goes for a drink.

Locate the following information.

5 The name of the Shakespeare play that Holden discusses with the nun.

6 The title of the record Holden buys Phoebe.

7 The name of the bar where Holden gets drunk.

Check your answers on page 89.

Consider these issues.

a Why Holden does not phone Jane Gallagher.

b Why the writer includes Holden's memories of his museum visits.

c The reasons for Holden enjoying his conversation with the nuns.

d Holden's behaviour on his date.

e The significance of Holden breaking his sister's record.

f How the writer brings our attention to Holden's worsening state of mind.

CHAPTER **21**

Holden arrives at his parents' apartment and explains that the normal elevator-boy is not on duty. He tells us this will allow him to sneak up and see his sister and leave without his parents knowing. Holden lies to the new elevator-boy, telling him he is going to see the people who live next door to his parents.

After getting into the apartment, Holden goes to his sister's room. He moves slowly and tells us that this is because his mother is a very light sleeper and also has trouble getting to sleep. When he gets to Phoebe's room, he remembers that she sleeps in his brother D.B.'s room when he is away and goes there. Phoebe is asleep so Holden looks through her school notebooks before waking her up.

Phoebe and Holden start talking; she tells him she is in the school play. He finds out from her that their mother and father are at a party. He relaxes and tells us he doesn't care if they come home and find him there. Holden tells Phoebe about the record and she says that she wants to keep the broken pieces, which amuses Holden.

Think of the reasons for Phoebe being so upset.

During their conversation Phoebe suddenly asks Holden why he is home early. She realises he has been thrown out of school again and gets very upset. Holden tries to reassure her, but she keeps repeating that their father will be very angry. He leaves the room to look for some cigarettes.

COMMENT

Holden's talent for lying helps him get into his parents' house. This is one of the only times his lying has a practical purpose; normally he does it just for fun.

Consider why Holden takes such an interest in his sister's schoolbooks.

We find out a bit about Holden's home and the family lifestyle. He also seems proud of his sister's schoolbooks. This seems rather strange given that he does not seem interested in his own schoolwork.

Y

REUNITED WITH PHOEBE

We get a strong impression of Phoebe's character from her conversation with Holden. She obviously cares for her brother. Her distress when she realises he has been thrown out of school is caused by her understanding that there will be resulting family arguments.

GLOSSARY   **plastered** drunk

CHAPTER 22

Holden goes back into the room to see Phoebe. She continues to ignore him and it reminds him of when the fencing team ignored him on his last day at Pencey Prep. Phoebe is still preoccupied with Holden being thrown out of school. Eventually Holden tries to explain to Phoebe why he did not like Pencey. He tells her it was full of phonies and mentions briefly how badly Ackley was treated there. He remembers Spencer and accuses him of sucking up to the headmaster and describes 'Veterans' Day'.

Consider why Holden has these particular memories of Pencey.

Phoebe tells Holden that he doesn't like anything and asks him to name something he does like. Holden tells us he can't concentrate and that the only thing he could remember were the nuns and an incident at Elkton Hills, one of his old schools, where a boy jumped out of a window to his death rather than give in to some bullies. Instead of telling Phoebe this, he tells her he likes Allie.

Phoebe continues to probe Holden about what he wants to be in life. Holden dismisses his sister's suggestions and goes on to ask her if she knows the song *If a body catch a body comin' through the rye.* She tells him it's a poem by Robert Burns and that it is 'meet' not 'catch'. Holden then describes to her an image in his mind of himself standing on the edge of a cliff, stopping children who are running out of a field of rye from falling over the edge. He says he would be '*the catcher in the rye*'.

Holden decides to phone his old English teacher from Elkton Hills, Mr Antolini. He leaves the room, telling Phoebe to stay awake.

COMMENT

During Holden's conversation with Phoebe we see that his younger sister is disappointed in him. Holden thinks that Phoebe will understand his feelings, but she is baffled by his behaviour.

When Phoebe challenges Holden to name something he would like to be he cannot do so.

James Castle will form an important link with Mr Antolini, a teacher who Holden respects and turns to for answers to his problems.

By mentioning Ackley and James Castle, the boy who died at Elkton Hills, the author reinforces our image of Holden as an outsider. His mind is filled with images of unwanted people during his talk with Phoebe. The things he 'likes' or, in other words, thinks are morally good, are not valued by society; examples are the nuns and the boy who dies rather than take back what he has said.

Give your interpretation of Holden's description of what he wants to be.

This is the only time in the novel the complete title, '*The catcher in the rye*', is mentioned. Holden's explanation of what he would like to be is completely unrealistic. But when we look beneath the surface of his description it seems to give us Holden's real dream. He wants to save others from what has happened to him. He feels that he has, in one way, 'fallen off a cliff'. He wants to protect children like Allie, Ackley and James Castle from the world.

GLOSSARY   **ostracising** ignoring
                Veterans' Day school reunion
                N.Y.U. New York University

CHAPTER 23

Give reasons why Holden keeps referring to his cigarette-smoking.

Holden phones Mr Antolini and arranges to go and see him straight away. Holden reveals to us that Mr Antolini was the person who finally picked up the dead boy, James Castle, at Elkton Hills school.

When Holden has returned to D.B.'s room, he dances to the music on the radio with Phoebe. He tells us that Phoebe is a good dancer. Holden sits down on the bed and tells us he is breathless, due to the number of cigarettes he has been smoking.

They hear the front door open and realise that their parents have returned home, so Holden hides in the wardrobe. Phoebe and her mother have a conversation, which involves Phoebe covering up for the smell of smoke created by Holden, and Holden is not noticed. Their mother leaves the room, saying goodnight to Phoebe.

Think about why Holden gives Phoebe his hat.

Holden borrows Phoebe's Christmas savings and tells her he won't go away until after her school play. He suddenly starts to cry and Phoebe tries to comfort him. Holden tells us he cried for a long time but finally gets his coat and gets ready to leave. Before he goes he gives Phoebe his red hunting hat.

COMMENT   Holden's remarks about Mr Antolini give us a clue about why he wants to see him. He is a figure of authority whom Holden thinks will help him. Mr Antolini is portrayed as a caring person who does not think about himself when helping others. This quality is similar to the nuns whom Holden admires.

Notice the contradiction in Holden's behaviour in this chapter. In Chapter 21 he told us that he didn't mind if

Y

his parent's 'caught' him and yet he hides from them here. It seems as if he is still too afraid to face their reaction to his expulsion from school.

When Holden breaks down in tears this is a sign that he feels he is letting his sister down. He feels that he has to run away and yet he is frightened of leaving the person he cares most about. Phoebe's willingness to give him her Christmas savings and the way she deceives her mother for him makes him realise he is going away from someone who genuinely cares about him.

GLOSSARY   **closet** wardrobe
                   garbage pails dustbins

CHAPTER 24

Holden arrives at Mr Antolini's house, telling us that he knew Mr Antolini well and explaining that he used to come and see Holden quite often.

Mr Antolini and Holden begin a long conversation. Mr Antolini asks Holden why he got expelled from Pencey, but Holden talks about why he failed the Oral Expression part of his English course.

Mrs Antolini comes in with coffee and says she is going to bed. After she has gone Mr Antolini tells Holden that he had lunch with his father and that they were both very worried about him. He says he feels that Holden is going to fail in life unless he starts to think about what he really wants to be and then applies himself to his studies. Mr Antolini continues talking, trying to explain what he thinks Holden is going through. During the conversation Holden has told us *What is your* he feels tired, and when he yawns Mr Antolini says he *opinion of the* will make up a bed for him on the couch. Whilst he is *advice Mr Antolini* getting it ready he asks Holden about Sally Hayes and *gives Holden?* Jane Gallagher. Holden says he will ring Jane tomorrow.

Holden goes to sleep but suddenly wakes up to find Mr Antolini patting his head. Holden becomes very disturbed by this and decides to leave Mr Antolini's house. Whilst he is waiting for the lift, he has an uncomfortable conversation with Mr Antolini.

COMMENT   During this chapter Holden has one of the longest conversations with someone in the whole novel. It is one of the only times Holden seems to be able to talk freely with someone. However, he does not feel well and it seems difficult for him to concentrate on what Mr Antolini is saying. He also comments quite frequently about Mr Antolini's drinking, making him appear not quite as stable and reliable as his conversation indicates.

There is a genuine feeling that Mr Antolini cares for Holden and is concerned about his future. He wants to work out what Holden is going through and we feel that he is the first person we have come across who comes close to understanding Holden's predicament.

Consider whether Holden overreacts to the situation.   The shock that Holden feels when he wakes up, and his reaction, seem extreme. He feels that Mr Antolini is making sexual advances to him. He says that Mr Antolini was behaving like a 'pervert'. Holden's perception of what has happened is that someone whom he respected and trusted has let him down. This incident is, in some ways, the final straw for Holden. The last person Holden turns to for advice and help seems to care about him for all the wrong reasons, as far as Holden is concerned.

At the end of the chapter Holden is out on the streets again and we feel that he is cast adrift from everyone he knows. The writer has created a real sense of foreboding for us.

CHAPTER 25

It is dawn on Monday as Holden leaves Mr Antolini's house. He goes to Grand Central Station (see map on p. 10) and sleeps on a bench until about nine o'clock. He reflects on what happened at Mr Antolini's and thinks that, perhaps, he should have returned to the house.

Holden wanders around the streets and tells us he was looking around for the two nuns he talked to the day before. Suddenly Holden has a frightening psychological experience: he keeps thinking he is going to disappear. To overcome his fear, he pretends to talk to Allie.

When Holden has recovered from the experience, he decides to go away, to hitchhike to the far west of the country. He gets excited about his journey and decides to go and arrange to meet Phoebe at the Museum of Art before he leaves, to return her money and say goodbye.

After leaving her a note he thinks about phoning Jane Gallagher but informs us he isn't in the mood. He goes to the museum. While waiting for Phoebe two small boys ask him if he knows where the Egyptian section of the museum is. Holden starts telling them about Egyptian mummies. The boys leave and Holden goes to see the mummies. Holden then goes to the toilet, telling us he feels ill. He passes out briefly but recovers.

There are clues through the novel that Holden is physically ill.

Holden goes back to the museum entrance and sees Phoebe across the street. She is carrying a large suitcase and, when they meet, tells Holden she is going away with him. Holden is shocked and tells his sister she cannot go. Phoebe starts to cry and Holden tells her he isn't going anywhere; he offers to walk her back to school but she tells him she isn't going.

Instead of returning Phoebe to school, Holden takes her to the zoo. They leave the zoo and Holden takes Phoebe to the park where there is a carrousel. Phoebe rides on the carrousel, putting Holden's hat back on his head before she gets on. As Holden watches Phoebe on the carrousel it starts to rain. He suddenly feels deliriously happy and says he doesn't know why. He just enjoys watching Phoebe on the carrousel.

COMMENT   In this chapter we have reached the climax of the story Holden wants to tell. He is physically exhausted, ill and unable to think straight. He has nowhere to go and his plan to go away to the 'wild west' is as unrealistic as his desire to be 'the catcher in the rye'. There is an increasing sense of desperation surrounding Holden's thoughts and actions.

By mentioning the mummies in the museum, the writer cleverly links the early part of Holden's tale with what is happening to him now. We recall Holden's failure in his History exam, part of the reason for being thrown out of Pencey and, therefore, part of the reason for his current plight.

Eventually Holden realises that he has to take some kind of responsibility when Phoebe insists on going away with him. He has learnt the lesson that what a person does always has consequences. He knows that he wants his sister to be happy and we feel that he cares for her more than for anyone else in the novel. He cannot even think about her accompanying him and therefore makes the decision not to go. His love for his sister has overcome his fear of facing his parents and it is perhaps this realisation that makes him so happy at the end.

GLOSSARY   **carrousel** fairground ride

CHAPTER 26

Holden informs us that he has told us as much as he wants to. He hints at what has happened to him since being in the park with Phoebe, saying he went home, became sick and was eventually put in the place from where he has narrated the story.

Holden tells us that he is going back to school in September, but is still unsure how he will behave when he gets there. He says he will try to apply himself.

Think of what Holden might mean when he says he will even miss Maurice.

He tells us that his brother, D.B., comes to visit him and has asked Holden what he feels about the story he has told. Holden says he doesn't know, but that he misses all the people he has talked about.

COMMENT   This final short chapter rounds off the novel. In some ways it is like the first page of Chapter 1, 'returning' the reader to the hospital that Holden is in. We feel a sense of relief that Holden is on the way to overcoming his problems, but there is also a feeling that there could still be trouble ahead for him.

GLOSSARY   **fall** autumn

A Identify the following characters.

1 The boy who died at Elkton Hills.

2 The character Phoebe is to play in the school pageant.

Locate the following information.

3 Where Holden's parents are when he returns home.

4 The name of the poet who wrote, *If a body meet a body coming through the rye*.

5 What Mr Antolini drinks.

6 Where Holden goes after leaving Mr Antolini's.

7 Where Holden and Phoebe go when they meet in Chapter 25.

Check your answers on page 89.

B Consider these issues.

a The reasons Holden gives to Phoebe for disliking Pencey Prep.

b Holden's relationship with Phoebe.

c The way the writer builds up Mr Antolini's character.

d Holden's reaction when he wakes up to find Mr Antolini patting his head.

e How the writer creates a sense of climax in the closing chapters.

f Why the writer ends Holden's tale when he does.

PART THREE

COMMENTARY

THEMES

All of the main themes in *The Catcher in the Rye* link
to Holden's personal experience of the world.
However, we can isolate four major themes in the novel.
These are:

- Relationships
- The Individual and Society
- The Effects of the Environment
- Innocence and Childhood

These themes interlink to influence and develop the
overall story of Holden's search for an answer to
his troubles and his descent into psychological
breakdown.

RELATIONSHIPS

Holden as an outsider

One of the main strands of the novel concerns Holden's
problems in forming relationships. In many parts of the
novel we find Holden telling us how lonely he feels;
this is shown by his increasingly desperate attempts to
befriend people. From the beginning of his story he has
problems getting on with others.

School

We first meet him when he has been 'ostracised' by the
fencing team. He is on his own when everyone else is
enjoying themselves at a football match. His
relationships with his schoolfriends are insecure: he
talks to Ackley but tells us he doesn't like him; he
admires Stradlater in some ways but ends up fighting
with him and leaving Pencey.

Adults and parents

The first adult we meet, Mr Spencer, cannot
understand Holden, even though he seems to like him.
The other important adult figure, Mr Antolini, also

cannot understand Holden. Even though he tries to give Holden advice about his life, Holden just feels tired and cannot really relate to what is being said to him. Holden's relationship with his parents seems distant, as if he thinks they do not really care about him. Holden's problems are mainly caused by his and his parents' inability to form a family relationship of trust and understanding.

Meaningful conversations

All through the novel Holden attempts to engage people of all sorts in conversation, but his only meaningful ones are with the two nuns and his younger sister Phoebe. Here he is being himself. Many of his other attempts at talking to others are characterised by him lying or pretending to be someone he is not. He lies to Mrs Morrow on the train and tries to be sophisticated with the three girls he meets in the Edmont Hotel. In New York he attempts to relate to people in what he sees as an adult way but fails again.

Relationships in the past

Holden tends to remember his relationships with people in his past more favourably. He speaks fondly of how he and his brothers were happy together as children. When he talks about his brother Allie we sense a closeness which is not there in his present life. His other really significant relationship was with Jane Gallagher when they spent one summer together. In a way this is the closest Holden has come to being in love. His failure to contact Jane when he is in New York shows how he cannot relate to anyone. He is frightened of spoiling the memory of a good relationship and substitutes her for Sally Hayes, whom he feels is shallow. He cannot relate to Sally and their brief day out ends in another failed relationship for Holden. He often talks about sex and mistakenly believes that this aspect of a relationship is the most 'adult' or important. This is a typical response for a boy of his age. Holden's inability to understand sexuality shows his immaturity.

THE INDIVIDUAL AND SOCIETY

Society and materialism

Much of Holden's story concerns his reactions to the values of the society in which he lives. He is disillusioned with his world and rebels against it. The society he lives in seems to him to be shallow and only concerned with material things; money is the most important thing and Holden feels this is wrong. This can be seen by the fact that the only two adults Holden feels empathy with are the nuns. Nuns have to give up material things and money; they take vows of poverty. They seem to Holden to be the only people he meets who genuinely care about others.

The values of school

Holden's dislike of his society's values can be clearly seen at Pencey, where he is very sarcastic about the school and its claims to 'mould' students into valuable members of society. School is normally where young people learn to become responsible members of their society, but Holden rejects the 'values' of Pencey just as he did the other schools from which he was expelled. Holden mocks Mr Ossenburger, someone who became rich after leaving Pencey, and says he is only regarded as important because of his wealth, rather than because he has done anything of value for others. All of the schools Holden has attended are for the rich and privileged. Many members of society would think themselves lucky to have these opportunities, but Holden seems to feel guilt and anger at his situation and rebels against it.

New York people

The social and moral values of the people Holden meets in New York are portrayed as either corrupt or petty and snobbish. The places Holden goes to in search of companionship are full of people only interested in themselves and how others see them. The piano player at Ernie's bar and the couple whom he meets there are examples of this. The prostitute and the elevator-man exemplify how corrupt society has become. In one of Holden's 'weak' moments he thinks he can buy the company and the experience he wants, but when he behaves as he thinks other adult men in his society behave this results in embarrassment and humiliation.

Pressure to
conform

Throughout the novel Holden is critical of the society in which he lives. No aspects of it seem worthwhile. The pressure which society puts on people to conform and be like one another puts an enormous strain on Holden. He is portrayed as an outsider who tries to fit in but cannot. This is the dilemma for Holden that leads to his breakdown.

THE EFFECTS OF THE ENVIRONMENT

The idea of environment affecting someone's behaviour is an important theme of *The Catcher in the Rye*. Holden moves through three main environments: Pencey Prep, the clubs, bars and streets of New York City (see map on p. 10) and lastly Central Park. They all have an impact on him and he tries to escape from all of these places at one time or another in the story.

Pencey Prep

At Pencey Holden is a part of the community, although he is on the verge of leaving. He deals with the people he comes into contact with on an equal basis. He is secure and confident at the school even though he tells us he does not like it and the environment there seems to stifle him. Holden views the school as boring, trivial and phony. Although it is his fight with Stradlater which finally makes him leave, we often feel Holden wants to escape from the confines of school. Holden cannot obey the rules and regulations which govern the boarding school environment.

New York

J.D. Salinger often makes the streets of New York seem a frightening place. One example of this is his description at the beginning of Chapter 12; another, in Chapter 25, is when Holden feels he is disappearing and that the city is going to 'swallow' him up. He will become one of the casualties of his environment, like many other city-dwellers.

Central Park   The park represents one place where Holden can find some happiness and it is here that his story ends. However, the park is also a frightening place for him and it is his fears in the park which lead to him going home at the end of Chapter 20. The park is still the place where Holden can be happy with his sister, perhaps because it has associations for him with his childhood, a more innocent and happy time.

Effect on   The different environments in which Holden finds
emotions   himself all contribute to his inner emotions:

- The museums and the park make him nostalgic and he wishes that time could stand still or even go backwards
- The clubs and bars bring out Holden's cynicism but also his insecurities and naïveté
- The city as a whole brings on Holden's depression
- The pace and confusion of city life reflects Holden's own confusion and fear

INNOCENCE AND CHILDHOOD

Transition   In *The Catcher in the Rye* Holden is at the age between childhood and adulthood. The difficulties he has making this transition are a principal part of the story; it is a type of story called a *bildungsroman* (see Literary Terms), but not a conventional one. Holden's development is twisted and he does not reach maturity by the end of the story. We also only find out about his earlier life in flashbacks (see Literary Terms).

In some ways Holden is afraid of growing up. He seems unable to face the responsibilities which come as he gets older. This is shown by his continued 'flunking' of his exams, even though he is obviously intelligent. His answer to his problems is a typically childlike dream, to 'run away' and have an adventure: he runs away from Pencey Prep and later talks to Sally Hayes and his sister Phoebe about escaping to the country.

Allie and Jane

Holden's happiest memories concern his own childhood before the death of his brother Allie. The only other time he has seemed genuinely happy since then is the time he spent with Jane Gallagher. These relationships were innocent ones, they happened before Holden saw how cruel the world could be. When his brother died, Holden's own childhood was lost and he had to confront something he did not understand; his reaction is extreme and marks the beginning of his problems.

His relationship with Jane was innocent. Even though they kissed, Holden informs us it wasn't on the mouth! They played games together, like draughts and golf. Holden does not want to let these happy memories go and he idealises his time with Jane. His reluctance to phone her reinforces the sense that he does not want to see Jane grown-up: his childhood memory would be shattered. This is also clearly seen when Holden fights Stradlater and becomes almost obsessive about what Stradlater may have done with Jane. He is afraid that, because of Stradlater, Jane may have lost a part of her 'innocence' and moved into the adult world.

Holden's
childlike
qualities

Holden's innocence and childlike qualities are exposed when he tries to act out his perceptions of adult behaviour. They all end in disaster or depression. His initial attempts to get alcohol are thwarted and when he does get served he gets drunk and breaks his sister's present. His experience with the prostitute shows his innocence regarding sex, while she provides a contrast to this innocence. She is roughly the same age as

Holden and her life is already corrupted by the world in which she lives. His rounds of the clubs and bars all leave him depressed.

Fantasy and reality

Holden's tendency to fantasise also emphasises his childlike behaviour. He often retreats to the world of the imagination when things in the real world become too much for him. Examples of this are when he pretends to be shot and his great love for books and stories. His fantasies of life in the Far West, or in the mountains with Sally Hayes, show he is unable to face reality and that he still has the unrealistic dreams of a young adolescent. Holden's admissions that he doesn't understand women and adults in general contribute to our view of him as immature.

Holden's quest completed

Holden cares about the innocent aspects of his world, which have not changed as he is growing up: the park, the children's zoo and the museums he visited. His sister Phoebe, still uncorrupted by the adult world, is the only person to whom he can really relate. It is the innocent image (see Literary Terms) of his sister on a children's fairground ride which finally makes him feel happy for a moment. Holden's quest is complete; he seeks refuge in the innocent pleasure of a fairground ride, rather than the adult world he has inhabited over the previous two days.

STRUCTURE

NARRATIVE STRUCTURE

The Catcher in the Rye is a story told within a frame. The story is of the three days of Holden's life between leaving Pencey Prep and going home to his parents, on to a therapist or doctor of some kind in a hospital in California. This frame narrative (see Literary Terms) is contained within the first page of Chapter 1 and the last chapter. The core of the story concerns what happened to Holden in New York, but this story also contains many flashbacks (see Literary Terms) to his childhood and to other events in his past. The novel is essentially episodic (see Literary Terms); it does not have a traditional 'beginning, middle and end' and progress strictly in an even time-sequence. Instead it relates various significant episodes in Holden's past and present life, sometimes jumping backwards and forwards, in order to build a detailed picture of a disturbed and confused young man who is heading towards emotional breakdown. There is, however, a definite structure to the novel.

The structure of *The Catcher in the Rye* is formed by four main sections as reflected in the Summaries. Each section has a climax which moves on the action and also reveals more about Holden's character and feelings.

Leaving Pencey Prep

The climax in the first section is Holden's fight with Stradlater, which drives Holden to leave school earlier than he had to. We also realise at the end of this section that there are people who Holden cares deeply about, for example his dead brother Allie and Jane Gallagher.

The Edmont Hotel

In the second section we have the disastrous climax to Holden's attempts at acting as a suave, young man on the town. This is his encounter with the prostitute and occurs almost exactly in the middle of the novel. It is a powerful episode, which makes Holden leave the hotel and also shows his vulnerability to the harsh, corrupt world of the city. At this point we also get a sense of how depressed and insecure Holden feels and we sense that something terrible will possibly happen to him.

Faces from the past

At the end of the third section, Holden has reached his lowest point and he returns home. This is a turning point in the story. Holden is frightened and alone, and, despite his efforts through this section to befriend people, he ends up drunk and alone in Central Park, looking for the ducks which Salinger uses as a symbol (see Literary Terms) of escape. Holden's problems in finding the lake are a device to show he has no escape-routes left. He has no options left but to return to his home.

Reunited with Phoebe   The end of the main tale is mysterious. The sudden ending with Holden's happiness at seeing Phoebe on the carrousel leaves us wondering about what happened to Holden when he returned home. The writer does not provide us with a closure (see Literary Terms) where the plight of the protagonist (see Literary Terms) is resolved. We have to form our own opinion of what happened next. The novel ends with us wondering if there will be a sequel, even though in the last chapter Holden says he wishes he hadn't started telling his story.

INTERNAL STRUCTURE

Although J.D. Salinger does not make extensive use of symbols (see Literary Terms), significant symbols are used to link important themes and ideas within the novel. For instance there are many circular objects which are associated with comfort, happiness and completion for Holden: the roundabout, the gold ring, Phoebe's record and Holden's red hunting hat (which also symbolises his individuality). Allie's baseball mitt is a relic of the past. Even certain characters represent specific values: for instance Jane symbolises purity and the untouchable innocence of childhood (see final section of Themes). Such use of symbols indicates how carefully *The Catcher in the Rye* has been structured.

It is impossible to give a description of every single person mentioned in the novel. Just as in real life, Holden has many chance meetings with people that are not that important to the novel as a whole, but which serve to increase the sense of real experiences (see realism in Literary Terms) we get when reading *The Catcher in the Rye*. The characters described here all have an important impact on the story.

THE CAULFIELD FAMILY

Holden Caulfield

*Witty
Sarcastic
Emotionally
disturbed
Disillusioned
Dissatisfied with
life*

Holden is the main character in the novel and we see the world through his eyes. He is a young man aged sixteen at the time of the events he describes to us, an adolescent on the verge of adulthood. Holden's language is meant to be typical of a teenager of the era and this defines his character for us (see Language and Style). He comes across as a witty individual who, nevertheless, can be irritating to those around him. He is from a stable background and his parents are quite wealthy; they live in an expensive part of New York. He has a younger sister and two brothers, one of whom is dead.

During the course of the novel we discover more and more about Holden's past and realise that he is a troubled young man. He is confused about much of the world around him and he is disillusioned with life. His sense of unhappiness and depression increases as the novel progresses, until he has a breakdown. It is left to the reader to decide whether this is because Holden is a 'weak' character or because he has experienced intolerable pressures and no-one has helped him to deal with them.

We are shown that Holden has a strong sense of moral values which often clashes with those of people around him. When he does things he knows are wrong he feels immediately guilty; all through the novel there is a sense of Holden's guilt about his behaviour and this is one of the main reasons he is afraid to go home to his parents.

Holden has a vivid imagination and a love of books and stories in general. Even though he claims to hate the movies, he spends quite a lot of time pretending to be in them! This frequent contradiction of himself is another of Holden's character traits. He tries to behave like an adult by smoking and drinking, going out with girls and hanging around in bars, but he is highly critical of others whom he sees living such a lifestyle and still yearns for his innocent childhood.

Phoebe
Caulfield

Pretty
Intelligent
Stubborn
Inquisitive
Loyal to Holden

Holden's ten-year-old younger sister is described by Holden as pretty, skinny and having red hair. Phoebe likes going to the movies and can tell a good film from a bad one. She is an intelligent girl with an inquisitive nature and has a love for writing stories. She seems to enjoy school and has lots of notebooks. Holden says she is a neat and tidy person and she seems very organised and 'grown up' for her age.

Phoebe becomes a very important character towards the end of the novel. For Holden she represents innocence and goodness and is a reminder of when life was happy at home. She is the main reason for Holden eventually going home. Phoebe becomes very distressed when she finds out that Holden has been expelled and this shows that she cares deeply about him. When he decides to go away, Phoebe insists on going with him. This also demonstrates the stubborn side of her nature. She is portrayed as a wise child, but one who still behaves in the manner which we would expect of a ten-year-old.

MINOR CHARACTERS

Allie Caulfield

Allie was Holden's younger brother by two years, who died when Holden was thirteen. Holden describes Allie as a popular and sensitive boy. Although he is not often mentioned he is an important character as his death could be what sparked off Holden's problems.

D.B. Caulfield

Holden's elder brother D.B. is a writer. He moved to Hollywood to write for the film industry, which Holden feels is a waste of his talent. He visits Holden at the hospital in California, where Holden is recovering as he tells his story.

Holden's mother and father

Holden's mother is mentioned briefly and is described as being highly strung, especially since the death of Allie. Holden's father is also only referred to in passing; he is a corporate lawyer who earns a high salary. Although they are discussed very little, they are important to the novel as it is Holden's guilt and fear of their reaction that prevents him from going home.

SCHOOLFRIENDS AND CONTEMPORARIES

Robert Ackley
Outsider
Irritating
Ugly
Unpopular
Lonely

'Ackley boy', as Holden calls him, is an important character early in the novel. He has the room next door to Holden at Pencey Prep. He is described as an unpopular boy. He is a senior pupil, but no-one seems close to him. He has acne and bad teeth and is a 'slob'. Holden tells us he was not liked by anyone, including himself, and he was prevented from joining various societies set up by the other boys. He is an outsider in many ways, just like Holden but for different reasons.

Although Holden spends a good deal of time telling us about Ackley's bad qualities, he is the last person Holden goes to see before leaving Pencey. Holden seems to realise that Ackley, like himself, has no-one with whom to identify. Ackley often tries to start conversations or make friendships with people but is shunned, just like Holden in New York.

Ward
Stradlater

Stradlater is another character who is important at the beginning of the novel. He is Holden's roommate and his senior. He is described by Holden as handsome and popular with the girls, someone who knows about the world and is sexually active. He has seduced girls in the past and Holden thinks he is one of the few students he knows who has actually had sex. Stradlater is portrayed as the 'model' for society's idea of what a young man of his age should be like. He has his faults but, by and large, his behaviour is that of a 'normal', well-balanced, American male of his particular era. The way Stradlater is represented allows us to contrast him with Holden and sharpens our sense of Holden being an outsider, unable to behave as society dictates.

Worldly-wise
Sophisticated
Well-built
Popular with girls
Mature?

He is particularly important in the novel because he is the person who causes Holden to leave Pencey early. Stradlater seems to be able to do the things that Holden wants to do but cannot. There is a feeling throughout the novel that Stradlater makes Holden jealous, particularly his relationship with Jane Gallagher.

Jane
Gallagher

Although we never meet Jane in the novel she must be included as a major character, as she occupies so much of Holden's thoughts. She is a sensitive girl with whom Holden spent a summer holiday two years before the action of the novel takes place. She is portrayed by Holden as his perfect companion and one of the few people with whom he has ever felt comfortable.

Jane is, indirectly, another reason for Holden leaving Pencey. He fights with Stradlater because he believes he has behaved badly with Jane. Throughout the novel Holden thinks of phoning her, but never gets to speak to her. It is as if she represents a beautiful memory for

Holden which he is afraid of spoiling, so he is unable to talk to her.

MINOR CHARACTERS

Edgar Marsalla
A boy who causes a disturbance at Pencey by farting in a speech.

Carl Luce
Holden's old student adviser at Whooton school. He meets Holden for drinks and we realise that Luce has become an adult who does not want to respond to Holden's immature questions.

James Castle
The boy who died at Elkton Hills School. He jumped out of a window rather than take back something he believed to be true. He is an important link between Holden and Mr Antolini.

Sally Hayes
One of Holden's old girlfriends whom he takes out one afternoon in New York. She is described as very attractive but shallow. She comes from a wealthy background and is happy with her life. Holden upsets her by calling her 'a pain in the ass' when she refuses to run away with him.

Sunny
The prostitute who comes to Holden's room at the Edmont Hotel. A young woman the same age as Holden.

AUTHORITY FIGURES

Mr Spencer

Holden's History teacher at Pencey Prep. An old man who was friendly towards his students, often inviting them into his home for hot drinks. When we meet him he is suffering from flu and Holden wishes he hadn't come to see him. He shows concern for Holden and cannot understand why he is failing so badly at school.

The main scene involving Mr Spencer is when he reads Holden's History exam paper to him, showing up its inadequacies. Holden feels that Mr Spencer is being sarcastic, but tells us that Mr Spencer felt badly about failing him in the exam.

History teacher
Near retirement
Concerned about
Holden

Mr Spencer is important to the novel as he is the first 'adult' we meet. He typifies the 'generation gap' and is one of many 'grown-ups' in the novel whom Holden wishes he hadn't started talking to! Although he is kind and caring, he cannot relate to Holden's feelings.

Mr Antolini

Mr Antolini is Holden's ex-English teacher from Elkton Hills school, described as the best teacher he ever had. A youngish man, not much older than Holden's brother D.B., Mr Antolini is married to an older woman. They live in an expensive apartment in New York and are friendly with the Caulfield family. He makes an impression on Holden by being the person who goes to pick up the body of the boy, James Castle, who killed himself at Elkton Hills.

Intelligent
Friendly
Concerned
Heavy drinker

Mr Antolini is the last person Holden goes to in his quest to find someone to understand and help him and who can relate to him. They have a long conversation, during which Mr Antolini is described as drinking quite heavily. Mr Antolini tries to get through to Holden that he may fail in life if he does not pull himself together and decide what he wants. He shows genuine concern for Holden and we feel he really cares.

When Holden goes to sleep at the Antolini's apartment he is woken up by Mr Antolini ruffling his hair; this is interpreted by Holden as a sexual advance and the last character Holden looks up to comes under suspicion for having false motives.

MINOR CHARACTERS

The nuns

Two nuns whom Holden meets in a station cafeteria. They are also teachers, one of them an English teacher. Holden has one of his few successful conversations with them and thinks about them periodically after their meeting.

Miss Aigletinger

One of Holden's old junior school teachers, who used to take them to the museums around Central Park.

Mr Thurmer

The headmaster of Pencey Prep.

Mrs Morrow

The mother of one of the boys Holden knew at Pencey. Holden has a conversation on the train with her, telling outrageous lies about what his schoolfriends think of her son Ernest.

Maurice

The elevator-man with whom Holden makes the arrangement to see the prostitute. He beats up Holden after a row about the money owed to the prostitute.

LANGUAGE & STYLE

NARRATIVE STYLE

The particular style of writing used by J.D. Salinger is crucial to *The Catcher in the Rye*. The novel is written entirely from Holden's point of view (see Literary Terms). We are asked to believe that Holden is telling his story to a doctor or a counsellor of some kind and therefore it is important that the language sounds like spoken English. J.D. Salinger uses language to bring Holden's character alive. Holden has many 'stock phrases', which are repeated throughout the novel to give an impression of a particular individual's speech style. He frequently digresses from the subject, as a person would when telling an oral narrative. This sometimes creates the impression that the novel has not been carefully structured, but this is probably intentional by the author and adds to the sense of realism (see Literary Terms). The narrative style consciously avoids many of the devices we associate with 'literature': there is little use of metaphor (see Literary Terms) and not much 'elegant writing' or detailed description of places or emotions and feelings. This style enables J.D. Salinger to persuade us we really are seeing the world through the eyes of a sixteen-year-old.

HOLDEN'S USE OF LANGUAGE

Swearwords   One of the first things we notice about Holden's use of language is his use of swearwords; although today they seem mild, at the time they would have been quite shocking. He uses the word 'crap' quite frequently and expressions like 'my ass'. He has a limited set of insults such as 'you sonovabitch' and 'you moron'. Holden does not like certain swearwords and spends time at the end of the story rubbing off graffiti, saying 'fuck you', from the walls of his sister's school.

Other
expressions   Holden has many other habitual phrases. He often uses the expression 'it really was' or 'I really was', as if he wants us to believe him but is afraid that we will not. His other main phrase is 'that kills me', usually used to indicate that something really amuses him. These and other expressions like 'phony' make Holden an individual with his own way of speaking, but they also echo the slang of the time.

Exaggeration   Another characteristic feature of Holden's language is his tendency to exaggerate. There are many instances of this in the novel and this is the main way in which J.D. Salinger portrays the humorous side of Holden's character.

Vague expression   The way in which Holden expresses his feelings and emotions is made deliberately vague by the author. Holden often says he doesn't know why he likes things or that he doesn't know why he said a particular thing to someone. He frequently tells us what he is thinking, but does not seem able to draw any conclusions from his thoughts. On a number of occasions his descriptions of what is happening to him emotionally are summed up in one word, 'stuff' and he tells us things make him sad or 'blue as hell' but he cannot articulate why. His inability to express his emotions clearly is very noticeable at the climax of his story when he is watching Phoebe on the carrousel. Holden tells us he is so happy but can't explain why.

AUTHORIAL INTENTION

The way in which J.D. Salinger reveals the world through Holden's individual voice is very clever. By giving Holden a limited ability to describe his world in a sophisticated way, he has made Holden seem even more like a real person. Holden is fixed in our minds as a mixed-up teenager who lacks the sophistication of an adult to describe what is happening to him. If we feel sympathy for Holden – and it would be cruel not to – it is the way in which he has told his story which makes us do so.

PART FOUR

STUDY SKILLS

ESSAY WRITING

Everyone writes differently. Work through the suggestions given here and adapt the advice to suit your own style and interests. This will improve your essay-writing skills and allow your personal voice to emerge.

The following points indicate in ascending order the skills of essay writing:

- Picking out one or two facts about the story and adding the odd detail
- Writing about the text by retelling the story
- Retelling the story and adding a quotation here and there
- Organising an answer which explains what is happening in the text and giving quotations to support what you write

....

- Writing in such a way as to show that you have thought about the intentions of the writer of the text and that you understand the techniques used
- Writing at some length, giving your viewpoint on the text and commenting by picking out details to support your views
- Looking at the text as a work of art, demonstrating clear critical judgement and explaining to the reader of your essay how the enjoyment of the text is assisted by literary devices, linguistic effects and psychological insights; showing how the text relates to the time when it was written

The dotted line above represents the division between lower and higher level grades. Higher-level performance begins when you start to consider your response as a reader of the text. The highest level is reached when you offer an enthusiastic personal response and show how this piece of literature is a product of its time.

Coursework Set aside an hour or so at the start of your work to plan.
essay
- List all the points you feel are needed to cover the task. Collect page references of information and quotations that will support what you have to say. A helpful tool is the highlighter pen: this saves painstaking copying and enables you to target precisely what you want to use.
- Focus on what you consider to be the main points of the essay. Try to sum up your argument in a single sentence, which could be the closing sentence of your essay. Depending on the essay title, it could be a statement about a character: Phoebe is the character who saves Holden from himself, because she shows him the importance and beauty of childhood and because she is determined to stay with him when he threatens to run away; an opinion about setting: New York is used to show what is corrupt and wrong with the values of the society which Holden inhabits; or a judgement on a theme: One of the central themes in *The Catcher in the Rye* is the importance of relationships, as Holden spends nearly all of his time trying to find meaningful relationships to take the place of the ones he has lost.
- Make a short essay plan. Use the first paragraph to introduce the argument you wish to make. In the following paragraphs develop this argument with details, examples and other possible points of view. Sum up your argument in the last paragraph. Check you have answered the question.
- Write the essay, remembering all the time the central point you are making.
- On completion, go back over what you have written to eliminate careless errors and improve expression. Read it aloud to yourself or to a relative or friend.

If you can, try to type your essay using a word processor. This will allow you to correct and improve your writing without spoiling its appearance.

Examination essay

The essay written in an examination often carries more marks than the coursework essay even though it is written under considerable time pressure.

In the revision period build up notes on various aspects of the text you are using. Fortunately, in acquiring this set of York Notes on *The Catcher in the Rye*, you have made a prudent beginning! York Notes are set out to give you vital information and help you to construct your personal overview of the text.

Make notes with appropriate quotations about the key issues of the set text. Go into the examination knowing your text and having a clear set of opinions about it.

In most English Literature examinations you can take in copies of your set books. This in an enormous advantage although it may lull you into a false sense of security. Beware! There is simply not enough time in an examination to read the book from scratch.

In the examination

- Read the question paper carefully and remind yourself what you have to do.
- Look at the questions on your set texts to select the one that most interests you and mentally work out the points you wish to stress.
- Remind yourself of the time available and how you are going to use it.
- Briefly map out a short plan in note form that will keep your writing on track and illustrate the key argument you want to make.
- Then set about writing it.
- When you have finished, check through to eliminate errors.

To summarise: these are the keys to success

- **Know the text**
- **Have a clear understanding of and opinions on the storyline, characters, setting, themes and writer's concerns**
- **Select the right material**
- **Plan and write a clear response, continually bearing the question in mind**

A typical essay question on *The Catcher in the Rye* is followed by a sample essay plan in note form. This does not present the only answer to the question, merely one answer. Do not be afraid to include you own ideas, and leave out some of those in the sample! Remember, it is essential to use material from the novel to prove and illustrate the points you make.

What do you think are the reasons for Holden's breakdown?

Introduction

Holden tells us about his current circumstances and we realise he has a problem. Outline Holden's worsening condition as his story develops.

Part 1: Pencey Prep

- Holden is presented as someone who does not fit in. He has been expelled from school – the beginning of his problems.
- Describe his inability to apply himself to schoolwork and his lack of real friends in the school.
- Mention his brother Allie's death and the effects this may have had on Holden.
- Mention the fight with Stradlater and how it indicates his anger at the world in which he lives.

Part 2: Attitudes to people

- Outline Holden's attitude towards the people he meets, particularly his tendency to think of people as phony.
- Discuss Holden's loneliness and how he becomes depressed by people's behaviour.
- Comment on how Holden is alienated from people around him and the effect this may have on his mental state.

Part 3: Attitudes towards society

- Holden cannot understand the way society seems to work and feels that there is much unfairness in the world.
- Mention his feelings about religion and the fact that society seems hypocritical.
- Discuss how this may contribute to Holden's mental state.

Part 4: Guilt
- Holden feels guilt about many things he does.
- Discuss his feelings about his parents and their reaction to his expulsion from yet another school.
- Mention his attempts to behave like an adult and his inability to do so.
- Comment on his relationship with his sister and her fears about him.

Part 5:
Conclusion
- Life seems pointless to him after the death of his brother.
- He could not reconcile this with the demands people placed on him. Everything else seemed unimportant or shallow to him.
- What caused his breakdown was people's expectations of him.
- His worsening mental state is mirrored in the novel by his worsening material state, i.e. running out of money, sleeping rough, getting drunk.
- The emotional turmoil Holden experiences is responsible for his breakdown. This is the main reason for his stay in the hospital in California.
- The lasting impression is that Holden went through a period of his life where he could not cope with the pressures of growing up.

FURTHER QUESTIONS

Make a plan as shown above and attempt these questions.

1 What does the novel tell us about school?
2 How does Holden's way of telling his story affect our response?
3 Holden tries hard to act 'grown up' in the novel. Does he succeed?
4 Why is Jane Gallagher an important character in the novel?

CULTURAL CONNECTIONS

BROADER PERSPECTIVES

Teenage
rebellion

The Catcher in the Rye is a novel which is essentially about a young person's rebellion against what he sees as false values in the society around him. This theme continued through the literature, films and music of America in the 1950s; many early pop stars like Elvis Presley were thought of as dangerous and likely to corrupt the nation's youth!

This concept of youthful rebellion endures to the present day and many people talk about a gap between young people's experiences of the world and those of their parents. One of the most extreme examples today is the cartoon *Beavis and Butthead*, which shows two mindless teenagers who cannot understand the adult world around them and who engage in extremely anti-social behaviour. Holden is mild compared to these two! However, when the novel was written Holden's language and behaviour would have been regarded in much the same way as we see Beavis and Butthead's today. The difference is that Holden is intelligent and has his ideas of what is wrong with the world.

Links with
other texts

Many other writers also develop character by their use of an individual style of language; one example is *Huckleberry Finn* by Mark Twain. This classic nineteenth-century American novel creates a real and believable character for us: Huckleberry Finn is a likeable rogue who, in his own way, also rebels against his society's values.

Another book which caught the attention of young people all over the western world, published some six years after *The Catcher in the Rye*, was Jack Kerouac's *On the Road.* Like Holden, Kerouac's main character, Sal Paradise, is also an anti-hero (see Literary Terms), rebellious and restless. He is a more adult figure than Holden, but also is searching for some meaning to his life, and his story is told in a unique style just like Holden's.

Links with Cinema Many films concern similar issues to *The Catcher in the Rye*; the famous 1950s film *Rebel Without a Cause* also deals with a young man's problems and inability to fit in and find value in the world in which he lives. A film which helps to convey the stifling atmosphere of an American private school is *Dead Poets' Society*; however in this film it is the teacher who questions the accepted order; he is reminiscent of Mr Antolini in *The Catcher in the Rye*.

J.D. Salinger's book *Seymour: An Introduction* is interesting to read from the point of view of character and to help us understand J.D. Salinger's view of the world. Seymour echoes aspects of Holden Caulfield.

anti-hero an unheroic protagonist of a play or novel; a character whose attractiveness or interest consists of their inability to perform deeds of bravery or courage. Do not let the term 'anti' suggest to you that they are necessarily bad

bildungsroman a novel which describes the main character's development from childhood to maturity, focusing on the relationship between experience, education, character and identity

closure the impression of completeness and finality achieved by the ending of some literary works, for example 'they lived happily ever after' and 'Reader, I married him'. *The Catcher in the Rye*, like many other twentieth-century novels, has an 'open' ending which refuses to leave the reader comfortably satisfied and leaves the text open to multiple interpretations

episodic a type of narrative which is written in the simple form of a series of more or less separable or discrete episodes or incidents, rather than a complicated and involved plot

first-person narrative a story told in the first-person singular (an 'I' figure who is directly involved)

flashback a sudden jump backwards in time to an earlier episode, giving the reader a fuller picture as the past is described as well as the present. This term is borrowed from films – perhaps demonstrating Holden's familiarity with the cinema?

frame narrative the outer, containing story, which is a pretext for the more significant narrative embedded within it

image something described by the writer to create a particular mental impression in the reader

metaphor one thing described as another thing, thus 'carrying over' its associations

point of view the way in which the narrator approaches his or her material (characters, action, setting etc.) and audience

protagonist the leading character (or characters) in a novel or play

realism in literature, writing in such a way that represents things as common sense perceives them to be. Realism focuses on individuals rather than stereotypes

symbol something which represents something else by analogy or association. Holden's red hunting hat has symbolic value in *The Catcher in the Rye* (see Structure)

TEST ANSWERS

TEST YOURSELF (Chapters 1–7)

A
...
1 Mr Spencer
2 Mal Brossard and Robert Ackley
3 Three
4 Edgar Marsalla farting
5 His brother Allie's baseball mitt
6 Because of his bad health and personal habits
7 Because Stradlater complains about the essay Holden has written, then attacks his personality, and finally aggravates Holden by not revealing details about his date with Jane Gallagher

TEST YOURSELF (Chapters 8–14)

A
...
1 Mrs Morrow
2 Bernice, Marty and Laverne
3 Ernie
4 Sunny
5 The Lavender Room and Ernie's
6 Maine
7 An argument over money

TEST YOURSELF (Chapters 15–20)

A
...
1 Sally Hayes
2 Miss Aigletinger
3 The Lunts
4 Carl Luce
5 *Romeo and Juliet*
6 *Little Shirley Beans*
7 The Wicker Bar

TEST YOURSELF (Chapters 21–26)

A
...
1 James Castle
2 Benedict Arnold
3 A party in Norwalk, Connecticut
4 Robert Burns
5 Highballs
6 Grand Central Station
7 The zoo and the park

GCSE and equivalent levels (£3.50 each)

Harold Brighouse
Hobson's Choice

Charles Dickens
Great Expectations

Charles Dickens
Hard Times

George Eliot
Silas Marner

William Golding
Lord of the Flies

Thomas Hardy
The Mayor of Casterbridge

Susan Hill
I'm the King of the Castle

Barry Hines
A Kestrel for a Knave

Harper Lee
To Kill a Mockingbird

Arthur Miller
A View from the Bridge

Arthur Miller
The Crucible

George Orwell
Animal Farm

J.B. Priestley
An Inspector Calls

J.D. Salinger
The Catcher in the Rye

William Shakespeare
Macbeth

William Shakespeare
The Merchant of Venice

William Shakespeare
Romeo and Juliet

William Shakespeare
Twelfth Night

George Bernard Shaw
Pygmalion

John Steinbeck
Of Mice and Men

Mildred D. Taylor
Roll of Thunder, Hear My Cry

James Watson
Talking in Whispers

A Choice of Poets

Nineteenth Century Short Stories

Poetry of the First World War

Advanced level (£3.99 each)

Margaret Atwood
The Handmaid's Tale

Jane Austen
Emma

Jane Austen
Pride and Prejudice

William Blake
Poems/Songs of Innocence and Songs of Experience

Emily Brontë
Wuthering Heights

Geoffrey Chaucer
Wife of Bath's Prologue and Tale

Joseph Conrad
Heart of Darkness

Charles Dickens
Great Expectations

F. Scott Fitzgerald
The Great Gatsby

Thomas Hardy
Tess of the D'Urbervilles

Seamus Heaney
Selected Poems

James Joyce
Dubliners

William Shakespeare
Antony and Cleopatra

William Shakespeare
Hamlet

William Shakespeare
King Lear

William Shakespeare
Macbeth

William Shakespeare
Othello

Mary Shelley
Frankenstein

Alice Walker
The Color Purple

John Webster
The Duchess of Malfi

FUTURE TITLES IN THE YORK NOTES SERIES

Chinua Achebe
Things Fall Apart

Edward Albee
Who's Afraid of Virginia Woolf?

Jane Austen
Mansfield Park

Jane Austen
Northanger Abbey

Jane Austen
Persuasion

Jane Austen
Sense and Sensibility

Samuel Beckett
Waiting for Godot

John Betjeman
Selected Poems

Robert Bolt
A Man for All Seasons

Charlotte Brontë
Jane Eyre

Robert Burns
Selected Poems

Lord Byron
Selected Poems

Geoffrey Chaucer
The Franklin's Tale

Geoffrey Chaucer
The Knight's Tale

Geoffrey Chaucer
The Merchant's Tale

Geoffrey Chaucer
The Miller's Tale

Geoffrey Chaucer
The Nun's Priest's Tale

Geoffrey Chaucer
The Pardoner's Tale

Geoffrey Chaucer
Prologue to the Canterbury Tales

Samuel Taylor Coleridge
Selected Poems

Daniel Defoe
Moll Flanders

Daniel Defoe
Robinson Crusoe

Shelagh Delaney
A Taste of Honey

Charles Dickens
Bleak House

Charles Dickens
David Copperfield

Charles Dickens
Oliver Twist

Emily Dickinson
Selected Poems

John Donne
Selected Poems

Douglas Dunn
Selected Poems

George Eliot
Middlemarch

George Eliot
The Mill on the Floss

T.S. Eliot
The Waste Land

T.S. Eliot
Selected Poems

Henry Fielding
Joseph Andrews

E.M. Forster
Howards End

E.M. Forster
A Passage to India

John Fowles
The French Lieutenant's Woman

Elizabeth Gaskell
North and South

Oliver Goldsmith
She Stoops to Conquer

Graham Greene
Brighton Rock

Graham Greene
The Heart of the Matter

Graham Greene
The Power and the Glory

Thomas Hardy
Far from the Madding Crowd

Thomas Hardy
Jude the Obscure

Thomas Hardy
The Return of the Native

Thomas Hardy
Selected Poems

L.P. Hartley
The Go-Between

Nathaniel Hawthorne
The Scarlet Letter

Ernest Hemingway
A Farewell to Arms

Ernest Hemingway
The Old Man and the Sea

Homer
The Iliad

Homer
The Odyssey

Gerard Manley Hopkins
Selected Poems

Ted Hughes
Selected Poems

Aldous Huxley
Brave New World

Henry James
Portrait of a Lady

Ben Jonson
The Alchemist

Ben Jonson
Volpone

James Joyce
A Portrait of the Artist as a Young Man

John Keats
Selected Poems

Philip Larkin
Selected Poems

D.H. Lawrence
The Rainbow

D.H. Lawrence
Selected Stories

D.H. Lawrence
Sons and Lovers

D.H. Lawrence
Women in Love

Laurie Lee
Cider with Rosie

Christopher Marlowe
Doctor Faustus

Arthur Miller
Death of a Salesman

John Milton
Paradise Lost Bks I & II

John Milton
Paradise Lost IV & IX

Sean O'Casey
Juno and the Paycock

George Orwell
Nineteen Eighty-four

John Osborne
Look Back in Anger

Wilfred Owen
Selected Poems

Harold Pinter
The Caretaker

Sylvia Plath
Selected Works

Alexander Pope
Selected Poems

Jean Rhys
Wide Sargasso Sea

William Shakespeare
As You Like It

William Shakespeare
Coriolanus

William Shakespeare
Henry IV Pt 1

William Shakespeare
Henry IV Pt II

William Shakespeare
Henry V

William Shakespeare
Julius Caesar

William Shakespeare
Measure for Measure

William Shakespeare
Much Ado About Nothing

William Shakespeare
A Midsummer Night's Dream

William Shakespeare
Richard II

William Shakespeare
Richard III

William Shakespeare
Sonnets

William Shakespeare
The Taming of the Shrew

William Shakespeare
The Tempest

William Shakespeare
The Winter's Tale

George Bernard Shaw
Arms and the Man

George Bernard Shaw
Saint Joan

Richard Brinsley Sheridan
The Rivals

R.C. Sherriff
Journey's End

Muriel Spark
The Prime of Miss Jean Brodie

John Steinbeck
The Grapes of Wrath

John Steinbeck
The Pearl

Tom Stoppard
Rosencrantz and Guildenstern are Dead

Jonathan Swift
Gulliver's Travels

John Millington Synge
The Playboy of the Western World

W.M. Thackeray
Vanity Fair

Mark Twain
Huckleberry Finn

Virgil
The Aeneid

Derek Walcott
Selected Poems

Oscar Wilde
The Importance of Being Earnest

Tennessee Williams
Cat on a Hot Tin Roof

Tennessee Williams
The Glass Menagerie

Tennessee Williams
A Streetcar Named Desire

Virginia Woolf
Mrs Dalloway

Virginia Woolf
To the Lighthouse

William Wordsworth
Selected Poems

W.B. Yeats
Selected Poems

York Notes – the Ultimate Literature Guides

York Notes are recognised as the best literature study guides.
If you have enjoyed using this book and have found it useful, you
can now order others directly from us – simply follow the ordering
instructions below.

HOW TO ORDER

Decide which title(s) you require and then order in one of the following
ways:

Booksellers
All titles available from good bookstores.

By post
List the title(s) you require in the space provided overleaf,
select your method of payment, complete your name and
address details and return your completed order form and
payment to:

Addison Wesley Longman Ltd
PO BOX 88
Harlow
Essex CM19 5SR

By phone
Call our Customer Information Centre on 01279 623923 to
place your order, quoting mail number: HEYN1.

By fax
Complete the order form overleaf, ensuring you fill in your
name and address details and method of payment, and fax it
to us on 01279 414130.

By e-mail
E-mail your order to us on awlhe.orders@awl.co.uk listing
title(s) and quantity required and providing full name and
address details as requested overleaf. Please
quote mail number: HEYN1. Please do not
send credit card details by e-mail.

York Notes Order Form

Titles required:

Quantity	Title/ISBN	Price

Sub total _____

Please add £2.50 postage & packing _____

(*P & P is free for orders over £50*) _____

Total _____

Mail no: HEYN1

Your Name _____

Your Address _____

_____

Postcode _____ Telephone _____

Method of payment

☐ I enclose a cheque or a P/O for £_____ made payable to Addison Wesley Longman Ltd

☐ Please charge my Visa/Access/AMEX/Diners Club card
Number _____ Expiry Date _____
Signature _____ Date _____

(please ensure that the address given above is the same as for your credit card)

Prices and other details are correct at time of going to press but may change without notice. All orders are subject to status.

☐ *Please tick this box if you would like a complete listing of Longman Study Guides (suitable for GCSE and A-level students)*

York Press

Longman

Addison Wesley Longman